T5-AST-423

Under the Lens

Under the Lens

A Look at the American Media

Teacher's Manual

Carol Keiser Bishop

Ann Arbor

THE UNIVERSITY OF MICHIGAN PRESS

Copyright © by the University of Michigan 1997
All rights reserved
ISBN 0-472-08429-1
Library of Congress Catalog Card No. 96-61724
Published in the United States of America by
The University of Michigan Press
Manufactured in the United States of America

2000   1999   1998   1997   4   3   2   1

No part of this publication may be reproduced,
stored in a retrieval system, or transmitted in
any form or by any means, electronic,
mechanical, or otherwise, without the written
permission of the publisher.

Contents

About This Book

Welcome to *Under the Lens: A Look at the American Media!* This book encourages students to explore the world of media and discover its impact on their daily lives. Media is an active, vibrant force in our society. It both reflects and shapes our images of the world around us.

The text is designed for advanced level students of ESL and has been taught successfully at this level. I have found that students respond well to the materials as presented in the book. However should you have access to samples of current media, I encourage you to illustrate the concepts in the text with these samples. Ideas of how to integrate current media into the course are suggested in the "Additional/Follow-up Activities" section of the teacher's manual, and the instructors who have piloted this course highly recommend their use. It is through actively involving students with current media that this course comes alive! (Note: The use of authentic materials in class is restricted by copyright. Instructors desiring to use authentic media samples should get permission from the copyright holders of those samples before using in class.)

As a teacher, you do not need to have knowledge of this discipline: this book should give you the information that you need. It has been piloted with teachers who have had experience with the topic and with those who have had none. One instructor had this to say:

> "I feel fortunate to have found a content text which consistently meets both content and skill objectives. The tasks are well balanced and promote development in a variety of skill areas. Each time I have used this text, students have said that the level of technical knowledge is challenging yet accessible for both those new to the field and those who have majored in communication/journalism in

their home countries. Although I felt I had little technical expertise in this area, the text and teacher's manual provided more than enough background information for me to guide the students with confidence. Finally, from a pedagogical point of view, the suggestions in the teacher's manual and the framework of the text serve as excellent resources for those who are relatively new to content-based instruction." (Aileen Gum, Intern, Michigan State University)

However, as with any content course, it is likely that you will need to research and familiarize yourself more thoroughly with the material than when using a traditional textbook that discusses topics like "holidays." Although the text and teacher's manual will provide the essential information to teach the course, I encourage you to do some background reading on the media (a basic freshman-level communications text is a place to start), as well as to be active in reading and watching for programs on the current media situation. The media love to critique themselves (witness the questions surrounding the cameras in O. J.'s courtroom), and it's easy to find issues of current relevance for your classroom.

Chapter 1 sets the foundation by providing a definition of media and describing its connection to communication in general. In addition, it explores the relationship between media and "real life." Chapters 2 and 3 continue to provide students with the language and the concepts necessary to discuss the issues that arise later in the textbook. Chapter 2 discusses "objectivity" and the ethics we expect the media to follow. Chapter 3 explores ideas of newsworthiness and discusses how that relates to the selection of the news on the part of news organizations. I recommend covering the first three chapters in order as the foundational ideas presented there build on each other.

The last three chapters cover three of the most accessible forms of media available to our students: newspapers, radio, and television. It is not absolutely necessary to cover these chapters in the order presented. However, be advised that these chapters proceed in logical order both from a content standpoint and a language standpoint, and some of the activities may rely on knowledge of information from previous chapters.

Each chapter finishes with an opportunity for students to interact with the concepts presented in the form of a journal entry. The journal suggestions are designed to help students synthesize the information given, and to bring their own experiences/opinions to the course. Teachers may use the journal section of each chapter as an individualized writing activity, or they may opt to instead use the journal suggestions as prompts for class discussions.

How to Use the Teacher's Manual

The teacher's manuals for the **Alliance** series were designed with two principal goals in mind: (1) to provide as much detail as possible for those teachers who are new to content-based language teaching (please use as much or as little of the information provided as you feel necessary) and (2) to develop an easy-to-follow format that is consistent throughout the text. This format follows that of the students' book and can be summarized as follows:

Opening Activity: This section describes the opening activity and its purpose.

Objectives for Students: This section parallels the "To the Student" section of the student's book but outlines both the content and language objectives for the chapter. You have the option of sharing the language objectives with the students.

Content Headings: The content headings follow exactly as they do in the students' book. Within each content heading, there are generally three sections:

> *Techniques:* For the relevant activities, the author will discuss the techniques, or approach, he/she has used to present the material to students. This discussion will be based on the author's actual experience and may or may not be used as a guideline for conducting the activity in class.

Answers and student handouts: Answers will be provided, as well as student handouts when appropriate. Answers will not be provided in cases where they may vary.

Additional/Follow-up Activities: Suggestions for follow-up, supplementary, or alternative activities are provided when applicable.

Scripts: All scripts from audiotapes (or videotapes) are provided at the end of the manual according to chapter, section, and activity.

I hope you find enough information here to feel confident in teaching the subject matter while feeling free to follow your personal teaching style. Suggestions are welcome and may be directed to Carol Keiser Bishop at Michigan State University, Room One, International Center, East Lansing, MI 48824-1035.

Chapter 1

Communication and Media

Opening Activity

The purpose of this activity is to get students thinking about the various forms of media and to identify their personal reasons for choosing one form over another. In addition, this activity prepares the students for the paired activity that follows. I have the students think about this question individually and then quickly move to the paired activity.

Objectives for Students

Content

1. Identify the different forms of media and discover their strengths and limitations
2. Provide a definition for media and the mass media
3. Describe a communication model and explain how media follows the model
4. Explain the relationship between real life and mediated reality

Language

Reading/Writing/Structures

Identifying referents; previewing; prediction; scanning; identifying paragraph focus; vocabulary in context; identifying contextual clues; journal writing (in response to ideas presented in the chapter)

Speaking/Listening

Listening for the main idea; listening for details; interviewing classmates; information gap presentation; lecture listening; group discussion

Chapter Activities

I. Examining Forms of Media

Techniques

Activities A and B are used as a first day activity. They help the class get to know each other and also focus the students' attention on the topic of media. They also move the class directly into activities C, D, and E.

C, D, and E are the different stages of a media jigsaw activity. The purpose is to have students examine a news story told by two different forms of the media and discover the limitations and strengths of each form. I particularly like this activity because it involves students in the media . . . they are discovering the concepts from their own experience.

Materials are provided at the end of this section to facilitate this activity. The materials include a newspaper article and a newsmagazine article. Generally this activity takes two days. Activities C and D can be completed the first day, and Activity E is done the day following.

This activity can be expanded to use other forms of media (e.g., radio, television, the World Wide Web) as well, making the comparisons of media even more rich. The expanded activity will require adequate preparation time and access to taping equipment. However, the extra effort is well worth it, as the activity is even more exciting and meaningful to the students when more forms of media are explored and when the news story chosen has current significance. The following paragraph gives information on how to go about collecting materials for an expanded activity.

I usually begin taping the radio and TV for current stories about two to three weeks before I conduct this activity. (This allows the newsmagazines the time to publish their story on the topic.) I also buy the daily newspapers that carry the story I choose. *A note of caution:* Be careful in choosing the story to examine. Stories that to us may sound interesting often carry too much background culture for the activity to work well. A simple story with little analysis works best (e.g., an announcement of a government official's appointment, a hurricane or other natural disaster, a crime event). However, any story that carries with it a lot of cultural knowledge *does not* work well (e.g., an abortion protest, an ongoing investigation, a political story that involves knowledge of personalities and their political stance).

Activity F encourages students to think about whether they find one form of media more credible than another. Such a discussion prepares the students for the reading passage in G.

The purpose of Activities G, H, and I is to provide students with another perspective on the strengths and limitations of the different media forms, and to give students practice in identifying referents. Activities H and I are appropriate for homework, provided that Activity H and the example in Activity I are addressed in class. I find that Activity I serves as an indicator of my class's reading proficiency. If students have trouble with the referencing activity, this textbook will be a challenge to them. (Not an impossible challenge, but the instructor will have to work to make sure the readings are understood.) Activity J is designed to test student comprehension and facilitate the integration of the information in the reading with Activities E and F.

Answers

A. Answers will vary.

B. Answers will vary.

C. 1. *Newspaper:* Mount Everest blizzard claims lives of climbers.
      Newsmagazine: Stories about victims and survivors of Mount Everest storm raise questions about the casual attitude inexperienced climbers bring to the climbing of the mountain.
   2. Answers will vary.
   3. Possible answers:
      Newspaper: Rob Hall's phone call to wife; names and ages and other personal information of climbers who died; Seaborne Weathers was rescued; Hall's and Hansen's plight and Hall's last words; information about normal weather conditions at the peak
      Newsmagazine: More details about how the victims died; stories of the survivors; details about climbers who pay to be guided up the mountain; details about the conditions during the blizzard; Rob Hall's phone call and conversation with wife; the Japanese/Indian expeditions; the helicopter rescue of Gau and Weathers

D. Answers will vary. (See differences in details listed in Activity C, number 3.)

E. Answers will vary. Possible answers include:

Form of Media	Limitations	Strengths
Newspaper	—can't announce breaking news —not as visually ap-pealing as TV —takes time to read	—more details are presented —cheap; accessible to most of the population —a "permanent" form of media . . . can be saved and looked at again —people with low lis-tening comprehen-sion can get the news
Newsmagazine	—can't announce breaking news —not as visually ap-pealing as TV —takes time to read	—more details presented —time to publish is used to gather analy-sis of the story —a "permanent" form of media . . . can be saved and looked at again —people with low lis-tening comprehen-sion can get the news

F. Possible answers:

I agree, because television allows me to see the event and make sure that the story is being reported as it is really happening. Or—I disagree, because whoever is holding the camera is filming his or her perspective of what part of the news event is most important.

H. Newspapers or television

I. 1. Newspapers; readers; what has been read; time to stop to think or rereading
  2. Radio's

3. People who listen to a particular program format
4. Credibility; factor; a particular source; people; a particular source; a particular source; the *National Review*
5. Media credibility; media; the information media contains

J. 1. Edelstein doesn't think that the issue of credibility is important. He instead prefers to focus on whether the different forms of media are useful to us in the same way or useful to the same kinds of people.

2.

Form of Media	Limitations	Strengths
Newspaper		—amount of information they can contain —readers can read what they want as fast as they want
Newsmagazine		—good content —interpretive reporting and analysis are used
Radio	—limited influence	—easy to use —easy availability —news is packaged according to the format enjoyed by the listener
Television	—viewers cannot rerun something they failed to understand —viewers cannot skip items of little interest	—lets people see and hear the news event for themselves —drama and excitement of the medium —some people prefer passive nature of the news

Material for Activities C, D, and E

See next page.

Near death, Everest victim called home

ASSOCIATED PRESS

KATMANDU, Nepal—In bitter cold and howling winds, with the peak of Mt. Everest just 500 feet above him, Rob Hall called his pregnant wife Jan on his fading radio to say goodbye. Hall, a 36-year-old New Zealander, had just reached the peak of the world's tallest mountain Friday, his fifth successful ascent. On the way down, though, he trailed others in the expedition he led in a futile effort to help 44-year-old Doug Hansen of Renton, Wash., who was ill and struggling. They were caught in a fierce blizzard that surprised a score of climbers Friday.

Hansen died that night. Hall offered false comfort to his wife. "Hey, look, don't worry about me," he said as the freezing mountain sapped the last of his life Saturday. On another section of the 29,028-foot peak, Seaborne B. Weathers, of Dallas, struggled down to about 20,000 feet and was plucked off Monday in the world's highest helicopter rescue.

"I'm OK. I'm better now," Weathers said as he arrived at the Katmandu airport, his face blistered by windburn, his hands crippled by frostbite.

Life and death, luck and chance. In all, eight climbers were believed to have perished over the weekend in one of the worst disasters since Everest was first conquered in 1953.

Yasuko Namba, 47, of Tokyo, was reported dead by another expedition member after becoming only the second Japanese woman to reach the summit.

Scott Fischer, 40, of Seattle, and Andy Harris, 31, of New Zealand, were presumed dead, as well as three climbers from India who ascended the Chinese side of Everest.

Although their deaths have not been confirmed, alpine experts said no one ever has survived two nights in the open without oxygen on the southern summit of the peak.

Hall and Hansen were trapped on the mountain without oxygen, fluids, a tent or a sleeping bag. Hall survived the night and was able to make a last call by satellite hookup to his seven-months pregnant wife at their home in New Zealand, a friend said Monday.

"Rob took the news stoically that rescue wouldn't happen until the following day, stating he would wait," said another friend, Guy Cotter, an expedition guide who had remained at a base camp. Others said Hall was experienced enough to know he was going to die.

"A bivouac without equipment 150 meters [500 feet] below the summit in bad weather means, at the very least, you're going to get frostbite, and it could go right through to death," said Peter Hillary, who climbed Everest with Hall six years ago. "He would have been aware of that."

Since Hillary's father, Sir Edmund, conquered it 43 years ago, the summit has been reached 629 times. More than 100 people have been killed, their bodies frozen and irretrievable in crevices or under snow or rocks.

Near the peak, most people need a tank of oxygen. Dehydration in the arid atmosphere can kill. High winds bring swift changes of weather, and temperature at night is normally 40 below zero.

Copyright 1996 the Associated Press. Reprinted by permission.

DEATH STORM ON EVEREST

A mountain that began to look easy kills eight

By DAVID VAN BIEMA

SEABORN BECK WEATHERS THOUGHT his chances of success were good. Mount Everest is a tough climb, to be sure, but not the monster it once was. Weathers, 50, a wealthy pathologist from Dallas, is not a professional mountaineer. But he was in the best shape of his life. He had clothing designed to protect him to 80C below zero. And he had paid $60,000 to Rob Hall—a renowned New Zealand climber and guide who had seen 39 people like Weathers to the top of the world in the past four years. "Rob felt we all had a very good chance of reaching the summit," Weathers would say later. "We had prepared correctly and were climbing at the right time. We knew what we were doing. What occurred later was really a total surprise."

Three days after Hall's optimistic assessment, Weathers, face burned black and arms nearly useless, would be one of the surprise survivors of one of the worst alpine disasters in recent memory. On the night of May 10 a storm swept the summit's fearsome "Death Zone" with snow, bitter cold and hurricane-force winds. Within 24 hours, eight of the more than 30 climbers on the peak were dead, among them Hall and Scott Fischer of Seattle, who was also running a commercial tour.

BY MAY 1996 EVEREST HAD BECOME THE accessible behemoth, or so it seemed. Never as murderously tricky to climb as K-2, the world's second-highest peak, its challenge lay in the brute facts of its extreme altitude, occasional storms and inaccessibility. As clothing and equipment manufacturers mitigated the first problem, and a sprawling base camp sprang up at 17,500 ft. to provide warmth and food to dozens of would-be peak beaters, the issue for elite climbers was no longer whether they could reach Everest's pinnacle but rather how many paying customers they could take with them. It was not exactly a risk-free ticket to Disneyland, but for less than $100,000 a wealthy and dedicated amateur could buy a decent chance at summiting: money could buy altitude.

Communications breakthroughs increased the impression that Everest was accessible to nearly anyone. Climbers call home from the summit using satellite phones. They send E-mail. Over the past two months, socialite-alpinist Sandy Hill Pittman has been describing her ascent with Fischer's group on the Internet and throwing in remarks about books and recipes. One of her cyber correspondents inquired as to whether there were "any permanent markers at the summit. Flags, or plaques, or anything like that? A gift shop, perhaps?" Pittman didn't tell her new friend that the most enduring mementos on Everest's higher reaches are the bodies of dead climbers. Weathers realizes that now. So do a lot of other people. Says Jeff Blumenfeld, editor and publisher of *Expedition News:* "You can be hooked up to a Website, you can call anyone on a sat phone, you can have the latest high-tech gear, and the mountain can still win."

MOST EVEREST EXPEDITIONS take place in early May, when the weather is best. Friday before last was temperate and clear, a day to rival the one in 1993 on which 40 people reached the top. Now 11 groups were swarming up the mountain's top 2,900 ft. like ants on a piece of cake. Fischer's and Hall's parties set out at around midnight and eventually merged, pushing together through waist-high snow up Everest's last couple of hundred feet. Despite delays due to the number of people crowding through narrow passes, the mood was good. The daughter of Washington State postal worker Douglass Hansen had earlier faxed in her support: "Come on Dad, do it." By 2:30 p.m., he and more than 20 others had reached the peak.

But as Jonathan Krakauer, a journalist covering the climb for *Outside* magazine, stood at the top of the world, he noticed something ominous: clouds were approaching from the valley below. Within two hours they had arrived and metastasized into a monster: shrieking winds blew sheets of snow horizontally at 65 knots. A "whiteout" dropped visibility to zero, and wind chill plunged to -140°F. "It was chaos up there," says Krakauer. "The storm was like a hurricane, only it had a triple-digit wind chill. You don't have your oxygen on, you're out of breath, you can't think." In one horrifying vignette after another, the mountain began picking off its conquerors.

The first to die may have been Yasuko Nambo, 49, one of Hall's clients from Japan; her frozen body was discovered the next morning, 1,200 ft. above the South Col, the valley between Everest and its neighbor Lhotse. Another guide, Andrew Harris, came within yards of the camp before apparently walking right off the 26,000-ft. Lhotse face. Fischer, a vastly experienced climber known as "Mr. Rescue," lagged behind his clients, perhaps to help stragglers. Searchers found him two days later high above the South Col. In the same area they found Taiwanese climber Makalu Gau, half buried in the snow and mumbling. Gau could be awakened, but Fischer was comatose; and so, by the stark rules of mountain triage, the overtaxed rescuers saved whom they could.

Leader Hall, meanwhile, had stayed on the ridge to tend Hansen, who had expended all his energy on the summit. Exposed and out of oxygen, Hansen died during the night. Hall hung on: at 4:35 the next morning, his startled friends in camp heard his voice on the two-way radio. Rescuers tried twice but failed to reach him: his only hope was to make his own way to the South Col. "We tried to get him to move," mountaineer Ed Viesturs told *Outside* Online. "And we thought he was moving down the ridge. But after three hours, he mentioned, almost casually, 'You know, I haven't even packed up yet.'" Instead, Hall asked to be patched through to his wife, Dr. Jan Arnold, back in New Zealand and seven months pregnant with their first child. They talked for several hours. Arnold had reached the summit with her husband in 1993; now "she was right there with him, basically," says a friend. At a press conference later, she reported that his final words had been, "Hey, look, don't worry about me." Then he turned off his radio.

On the northern approach to the peak, three members of an Indian expedition were stranded on their way down from the top. Their frantic comrades thought they had persuaded a late-departing Japanese group to forgo its summit attempt and stage a rescue. But when next heard from, the Japanese were announcing their successful climb. The appalled Indians believe the Japanese found all three men and left at least two to die. The Japanese called the allegations "contrary to the truth, onesided and unjustified." Responded an adviser to the Indians: "They [the Japanese] will have to live with their consciences."

THOSE WHO SURVIVED THE STORM HAVE THE choice of seeing their fate as either a happy accident or a miracle. Fischer's climbers, now led by guide Neal Beidleman, were saved when Beidleman glimpsed the Big Dipper during a storm lull and was able to navigate them into camp. Gau's sherpa managed to wake him and get him down to the high camp, where he could receive fluids intravenously. But the most remarkable revival was that of Weathers, the Dallas doctor. At 9 a.m. on Saturday, fellow climbers left behind his apparently lifeless body; that morning the news was relayed to his horrified wife in Texas. Later that day, she got another phone call. People in the high camp had been astonished to see a zombie-like figure staggering down the hill toward them, face blackened from the sun, arms held rigidly outward, eyes closed to slits. Weathers had refused to die.

Neither Gau nor Weathers, both in critical condition, would have survived were it not for Lieut. Colonel Madan K.C., a Nepalese helicopter pilot. Choppers seldom venture above 20,000 ft.: at a certain height, the thin air reduces their lift. Yet Madan flew up to a giant cross the climbers had painted on the Everest ice with red Kool-Aid. There he hovered, runners just touching the snow's treacherous surface, as Gau was loaded on board. Madan flew Gau down to the base camp, then repeated the process with Weathers. It was the second-highest helicopter rescue in history. By last Tuesday, when the survivors of the most disastrous 24 hours in Everest's history honored their perished comrades in a Buddhist service, NBC's Everest chat room had reported more than a million hits, including tens of thousands of condolence messages. Beidleman responded, "We haven't enjoyed the fact of reaching the summit. And we are still in grief."

The mountain no longer seems so accessible. Krakauer, one of the two survivors in Hall's summiting party, believes commercial expeditions "need to be reconsidered" both because the customers put the guides' lives in additional danger and because "when the s___ hits the fan, there is nothing any guide can do for any client." To which Sir Edmund Hillary, now retired in New Zealand, added, "I have a feeling that people have been getting just a little bit too casual with Mount Everest. This incident will bring them to regard it rather more seriously." —*Reported by John Colmey/Katmandu, Meenakshi Ganguly/ New Delhi, Jenifer Mattos/New York and Simon Robinson/Auckland*

Copyright 1996 Time Inc. Reprinted by permission.

II. Media and a Communication Model

Techniques

This section is designed to help students develop lecture listening skills. Activity A focuses on listening for the words or phrases that preview the material to come. The instructor can either use the accompanying taped version of the lecture introduction or use the tapescript to do it him- or herself. The purpose of Activity B is to expose students to an academic treatment of the definition of media and introduce them to one communication model. The questions provided in the text can serve as a listening guide to help students focus their attention on the main points of the lecture. Activity C is designed to help students apply the lecture concept of encoding and decoding to the problem of miscommunication.

The Twain fable (Activities D, E, and F) is great to illustrate the concept of decoding and its importance to successful communication. Students should *not* read the fable but instead should listen to it. Twain uses fancy vocabulary that could either raise student anxiety or demotivate students toward the activity. If they instead listen to someone who reads in such a way as to help carry the story line, they will get the main idea (which is enough to participate in the discussion). (Such a reading of the fable is on the tape.)

Activity D is designed to introduce students to the idea of fables and to have them begin to predict the personalities of some of the characters in the fable. If students have had no previous exposure to fables, encourage them to use a dictionary to find out what they are. In a heterogeneous ESL class, the chart concerning animal personality characteristics leads nicely to a discussion of how culture determines the attributes given to animals. Activity E is a listening guide to assist students in following the main story line. I usually tell students that the fable is difficult, even for native speakers, but they only are expected to get the main idea. Activity F allows students to integrate the communication model to Twain's moral and then extend the application to media in general. I usually have students do Activity F as a small group discussion. Question 1 may work better if the instructor first asks students to write a dialogue depicting the first interaction between the donkey and the cat. Question 2 is difficult, even for native speakers. It requires that the students negotiate the meaning between themselves. Generally, at least one student per group is able to help the others see the application, but occasionally it is necessary for the instructor to guide the students to their conclusions.

Answers

A. The definition of media and mass medium; communication: what it is, how it works, and how it relates to media

B. 1. An agency or means of communication
2. a. a mass medium must reach many people; b. it must make use of a technological device to communicate the message
3. Textbook (as stated in the lecture); other ideas could be the blackboard, an overhead projector (OHP), a world map, posters, newspapers, etc.
4.

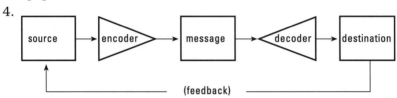

(feedback)

Figure adapted from the Shannon-Weaver Model of Communication, found in Wilbur Schramm and Donald Roberts, eds., *The Process and Effects of Mass Media.* Copyright 1972 by the Board of Trustees of the University of Illinois. Used with permission of the University of Illinois Press.

5. the miscommunication between the roommates regarding cleaning the apartment; the ESL teacher giving instructions; the child communicating that he or she wants down; the government agency communicating health-care information to a group of illiterate citizens

C. 1. E   We expect a company marketing in another country to do the research to avoid such blunders.
2. D   Charlene's life experience got in the way of her comprehension. Though she heard the message correctly, she didn't believe it because it seemed nonsensical to her.
3. E and D   The differing cultural values on both sides caused the misunderstanding.
4. Answers will vary. (It is helpful for the instructor to come prepared with a personal example to get the discussion going.)

D. 1. A fable is a short story that is used to convey a lesson (moral). Generally the characters are animals.
2. Answers will vary. Possible answers are:
Cat—aloof, regal; donkey—stupid, stubborn; elephant—wise, leader

E. 1. The cat, the donkey, the elephant, other animals
   2. The animals want to know what a picture is. The cat has told them of its beauty (and how it is enhanced by a mirror image), and they are curious to judge it for themselves.
   3. Every animal except for the cat made the mistake of standing between the mirror and the picture, thus seeing only an image of itself.

F. 1. The cat (the source) tried to describe a picture in a mirror (the message) by using many adjectives (the encoding) to express how beautiful it was. The donkey (the destination), due to his life experience of not ever seeing something so beautiful before, his doubting nature, and his haughty attitude toward the use of many adjectives in a description (all of which entered into his decoding process), decided to be suspicious of the cat's description (distorting the message).
   2. Twain uses this story of the animals as an allegory of what happens when people read a text. He believes that meaning is influenced by the mind of the reader, whether the reader is aware of his or her role in interpreting meaning or not.
   3. The author of a text (the source) encodes a message (the text) and sends it to the reader (the destination.) In order to gain meaning from the text, the reader must first decode it. However, because of each reader's individuality (background experiences, culture, personality), many interpretations of the original message can and will be made. Readers must be aware that they have helped to create meaning while in the process of reading (to paraphrase Twain's moral, they may not see their ears, but they are there).
   4. Media is no different from a text. The audience helps to create the meaning that they receive from a media source. Example: ESL students often complain that while they are at a movie, people laugh at things that they don't find funny. This is a case where one's culture or language skills limit the amount of the message that is decoded.
   5. Answers will vary. It is helpful for the instructor to come prepared with a personal example to get the discussion going.

III. Understanding Mediated Reality

Techniques

The text, "The Cone Effect: Understanding Mediated Reality," was chosen to provide a basis for critically evaluating examples of media throughout the course. The goal is to encourage students to view what they gain from media as a constructed package, designed to capture an audience's attention. Activity A is designed to have students begin to think about how media and society (or, as referred to in the text, "real life") are related. The opinions concerning this relationship are varied, and the discussion should bring out some of the range of opinions. Activities B, C, D, and E are previewing exercises. If students do them, they will find that the reading will go much more easily. I do Activities B and D in class and assign C and E as homework.

Before having students read the article, it may help to discuss the term *mediated reality.* I find it helpful to point out the relationship between a head noun and an adjective that is formed by a noun plus the suffix *-ed.* For instance, a *caffeinat-ed* beverage is one that has caffeine added to it. A *sugar-ed* tea is tea with sugar in it. A *pencil-ed* note is one that was written with a pencil. After observing these examples, students more easily understand the concept of "mediated reality."

Activities G, H, and I introduce students to the skill of identifying of contextual clues in guessing unknown vocabulary. The focus should be on finding the contextual clues rather than on guessing the vocabulary. My intent is to train students to be aware of such clues so that in other situations they are equipped to make good guesses. Activity H introduces students to the clues; Activity I asks them to identify the clues from sentences in the text and use them to determine the meaning of the highlighted vocabulary.

Activity J serves as a comprehension check for the reading. I have students do question 1 as homework and use questions 2, 3, and 4 to spark a class discussion. Questions 2 and 3 could be used as journal topics along with those in Activity K.

Activity K is meant to get students actively involved in the course by writing responses to the ideas covered. Research in writing across the curriculum has suggested that writing about a content area helps the student assimilate more of the content presented. Each subsequent chapter will also provide journal topics in response to the content.

Answers

A. Possible answers:
   1. Media shapes society. Look at the increase in violence in society. I believe the increase is linked to the incessant violent images people have seen over the years on television.

2. Media reflects what is already in society. The 1950s and 1960s stereotypical view of women was reflected in the sitcoms of that time: most women were cast as housewives.
3. Media both shapes and reflects our societal values. Sitcom images of how affluent families live are based on a segment of society that does exist. These images set a standard for those less affluent to try to achieve.

B. Possible answer: The article will show the relationship between real life and either constructed or perceived mediated reality.

C.

Paragraph	New/Previous	Focus Idea
1	N	Introduction to the article, the impact of mass media in our lives
2	N	Constructed mediated reality
3	P	Constructed mediated reality
4	P	CMR
5	N	Perceived mediated reality
6	P	Perceived mediated reality
7	P	Perceived mediated reality
8	N	Applying PMR to real life
9	N	Restatement of difference between mediated reality and real life
10	N	Concluding remarks

D. 1. *Mediamerica*/Edward J. Whetmore
   2. All life experiences that do not directly involve a mass medium
   3. Real life "blown up" by a communicator and transmitted in the form of a media message such as a TV show or magazine ad
   4. Perceived mediated reality is the audience perception of the constructed media message.
   5. *The Cosby Show, Miami Vice, Dynasty, General Hospital*
   6. "The Greatest Love of All"

E. Answers will vary.

G. *Glanced at:* to look at quickly without much thought
There is a contrast set up between two ways that we can look at a magazine ad. One way is to study it closely. We can infer that glancing at must be different than studying closely. In addition, glancing at is done as we turn a page. This phrase lets us know that glancing at is done quickly and without much attention paid to the magazine ad.

H. *Note:* the following are the best answers for the exercise. However, some of the sentences contain more than one type of contextual clue. I've included the additional acceptable answers in parentheses.

1. G; reporters or those gathering the news
2. B (C); not too wild or mellow . . . in between
3. E; interesting enough to be reported about
4. D; ABC, CBS, and NBC
5. A; means of communication
6. C; something done at the same time as another
7. F; truthful, keeping personal opinion out of one's reporting

I. The context clues used for each item are indicated in parentheses.

1. not ordinary/special (instead signals a contrast from the first sentence)
2. made larger/exaggerated (the reference word *this* showing that exaggeration was referred to in the previous sentence)
3. compete (the reference *such* indicates that the concept of competition is found in the previous sentence)
4. sent (the definition of *transmitted* is set off by commas; this is an appositive)
5. take (relationships: association; logical inference)
   compare to (relationships: association; logical inference)
6. making/placing (relationships: association)

J. 1.

Real Life	*Mediated Reality*
—ordinary relationships	—special relationships; those with intensity
—maybe one funny thing happens in one day	—dozens of funny things happen in a half hour
—ordinary people/ordinary lives	—people with special qualities or special events in their lives

—normal-looking people everywhere	—most people are attractive
—regular love affairs	—dramatic love affairs
—ordinary doctors	—doctors with an abundance of compassion
	—funnier, sexier, more intense, more colorful, and more violent
	—designed to attract an audience

2. Answers will vary.
3. Answers will vary.
4. This author probably believes that media and real life shape and mold each other. Although the media message always begins with real life (a reflection of society), the media message exaggerates the situation to gain a larger audience. This "blown up" feature can be perceived by the audience in such a way that it changes their ideas about how they look at real life (shaping society).

K. Answers will vary.

Additional/Follow-up Activities

1. After reading and discussing "The Cone Effect: Understanding Mediated Reality," bring in video clips of different types of television shows (e.g., drama, suspense, comedy, etc.). Have students identify techniques that the producers used to "blow up" real life: make it more exciting, attractive, etc. Sometimes it helps students if you turn down the sound or blacken the picture so they can concentrate on the audio and visual techniques separately. Students usually notice the following: laugh tracks, background music to set the mood, exaggerated expressions, camera techniques of softening filters, etc., flashbacks to other scenes, quick cuts to other camera perspectives, etc.

Chapter 2

Societal Expectations of the Media

Opening Activity

The purpose of this activity is to expose students to three different functions of the media. As a follow-up activity, you may want to ask students to brainstorm other functions of the media.

Answers

To entertain, B; to inform, A; to persuade, C

Objectives for Students

Content

1. Articulate the role or function of media in society
2. Explain why objectivity is difficult to achieve
3. Identify rules that society expects the media to follow
4. Analyze recent media decisions in terms of these rules

Language

Reading/Writing/Structures

Previewing; prediction; identifying main ideas; identifying supporting examples; critical thinking activities; vocabulary in context; identifying synonyms and hyponyms; scanning; reading for a purpose; summary writing; journal writing (in response to ideas presented in the chapter)

Speaking/Listening

Listening for gist; group discussion

Chapter Activities

I. The Function of Media

Techniques

Activity A is used as a prereading activity for the passage. I have used the discussion as a way for students to brainstorm the different expectations that they have for the media. Usually students not only focus on *what* media does for society, they also identify *how* media should go about carrying out their job. (Issues of objectivity, truth, propaganda, privacy issues, etc., come up in this discussion.) I encourage this line of thought as it ties nicely to the rest of the chapter. Activities B and C can be covered in class or assigned for homework.

Activity D involves critical thinking on the part of the students. Not only do they have to understand each quote, they then have to be able to identify the role that media plays for the person making the quote. Instructors have found that giving this activity as homework allows students the time they need to work on comprehending the quotes.

Answers

A. Answers will vary.

C. *The watcher:* to inform the public of important and relevant events and problems; to seek out and report situations important to the people (news)

The teacher: to teach people about matters necessary or useful about society's traditions, norms, attitudes (communicate societal norms/culture)

The forum: to build support for ideas and activities (persuade), uphold current values, or facilitate social change

Other functions: to entertain, to make money

D. *Churchill:* Media is a watchdog . . . (implied), keeps watch over corruption in government that could end up taking away the freedoms of the citizenry.

Jefferson: Media is a system of checks against a too powerful government.

Agnew: Media is a powerful machine that can influence government by their selection of stories and how they choose to tell the stories they cover.

Simons: Media is to report on *all* that is going on (not just that which sells the news), so that the people are better informed and can therefore better play their role as citizens.

Hart: Media is to carefully expose all aspects of government to be sure that government is performing its role as servant of the people.

Additional/Follow-up Activities

1. Have students examine a form of media for its various functions. *Example:* take a sitcom and examine the messages in it concerning societal traditions, norms, and prevailing attitudes. What societal norms does it assume? What societal norms is it trying to affirm or change? Obviously, it is meant to entertain and make money . . . but chances are it is also fulfilling other functions as well.

II. Objectivity

Techniques

Activity A is meant to get students thinking about the issue of selection and how this relates to objectivity. Media consumers need to recognize that any story they read or hear has been selected out of hundreds of stories . . . and the aspects of the story read or heard have been selected out of the original news event. I find it fun to have students keep their books closed at first, give each person in a group of four one of the cartoon frames, and have the student groups try to reconstruct the correct order of the cartoon story. This causes them to have to negotiate the meaning of the cartoon with each other. Activity B is a prediction exercise for the reading to follow. Students often can come up with some of the reasons described in the text from their own world knowledge.

Activities C and D are designed to have students focus on the aspects of the formatting of a text. An author uses formatting as a tool to help readers focus in on his or her message. In this case, students are to analyze the author's use of italics. The ensuing discussion in Activity E of the role of a "gatekeeper" in normal situations will help students better understand the media's usage of the term.

Activity G is meant to have students identify the main ideas of the reading and then apply their knowledge to the cartoon. Activities H and I require students to identify an author's use of supporting examples. The instructor may want to elaborate on this by asking students to think of other examples that would support each main idea.

Answers

A. Calvin is selecting what he wants his audience to see. Perhaps photo-journalists don't have the goal of "manipulating the truth," as Calvin does, but they have to select what to put in the frame of their camera, thereby cropping out part of the story. So too with reporters . . . they must select what will go into the limits of their medium, thereby deleting portions of the original news event.

B. Answers will vary.

C. talk, read, gatekeepers; answers will vary

D. talk: 4; read: 4; gatekeepers: 2

E. A gatekeeper allows certain people in and keeps other people out of a certain place. In the media industry, a gatekeeper allows some stories (or aspects of a story) into the paper or broadcast and decides not to run other stories.

G. 1. (1) An event described by media is not the original event but a constructed mediated reality—the event is selected and condensed from the original; (2) reported events are often taken from one medium and put into another (example of speech put into print), causing differences from the original; (3) reporters bring their own perspective to a story (their perspective affects how they "see" an event); (4) gatekeepers affect the selection and final choices of a story.

2. Reason 1 or 4: Calvin is selecting the portion of the story he wants the audience to see. He is functioning as a gatekeeper (who has an agenda!).

H. The author makes use of examples that the reader can identify with (suggesting the experiment of taping one's conversation and transcribing it), examples that refer to common knowledge (the politician "taken out of context") and examples of different kinds of gatekeepers.

I.

Reason Why Objectivity Is a Myth	Supporting Example(s)
The event described in a newspaper story is not the original event; it is a CMR.	—newspaper story is selective, condensed version of the original event —speech quotes taken out of context may appear absurd or sensational, resulting in irritated politicians
Reported events are often taken from one medium and put into another (example of speech put into print), causing differences from the original.	—a speech: given orally, reported in print —example of transcribing a conversation and the differences in how it seems when the conversation is read
Reporters bring their own perspective to a story (their perspective affects how they "see" an event).	—no examples are given . . . the author elaborates on his main idea (restates it) but doesn't give an example to support it
Gatekeepers affect the selection and final choices of a story.	—definition of gatekeeper is given, then many examples of different gatekeepers and the roles they play: news editors (choose the stories and their prominence); layout editors (decide length of story and if photo will accompany it); copy editors (rewrite story for easier comprehension, write headlines); photographers (their picture tells a "different story" than the reporter tells)

Additional/Follow-up Activities

1. Set up a situation so that the students "experience" the dilemma reporters have in maintaining their objectivity. For example: While your attention is at the blackboard, have a friend walk into your class, do something with your belongings, and walk out. Pretend you don't know who it was or what he or she did. Ask students to describe the person and tell what he or she did. The eyewitness accounts will most likely be

very different. (Some students will interpret the event, using words that indicate their interpretation . . . "the person *stole* your notebook.") 'Fess up to the experiment and then debrief by discussing why the accounts were different.

2. Examine articles or news programs that approach the news story with a bias. Have students identify the bias, explain how they know the bias of the piece, and brainstorm how the story would have looked if the bias had been opposite. (*60 Minutes, Dateline,* etc., stories are perfect for this. They appear to be giving the audience "news." But what they don't report in the story is very telling [who they don't interview, etc.] as to their level of objectivity.)

III. The "Rules" of the Media Industry

Techniques

The activities and materials of this section of the chapter are chosen to facilitate student *discovery* of the "rules" that we expect the media to follow. This section by no means thoroughly discusses the issue. Instead, it exposes students to some of the rules and encourages them to be thinking about other expectations that they hold of the media.

Activities A, B, and C are designed to get students thinking about some of their expectations of the media. In doing the tasks, they will identify two rules that they expect the media to follow. Activity A deals with the use of sensational news material that may "sell" the news but is in poor taste. Activities B and C deal with the issue of the personal privacy of individuals . . . and how this privacy is invaded if one is a public figure. I have found that the "Bizarro" cartoon is lost on some of the students if they aren't first asked to answer the questions in Activity B. Once the cartoon is understood, a class discussion can ensue regarding what is permitted in the news in their countries. Does the press in their countries report on the private lives of citizens? of public figures? Does a public figure give up his or her privacy after becoming famous? Would a news organization show someone being shot? the carnage of a plane crash? etc.

Activity D is a previewing activity based on the title, subtitle, and picture captions of the reading. A discussion of idiomatic expressions (e.g., to step over the line, to fall on your face, to backpedal, etc.) will assist the students in making their predictions of the article content.

Activity E is a vocabulary in context activity using a summary of the *Time* article, "When Reporters Break the Rules," as a text. The purpose is twofold: to continue developing the skill of identifying and using contextualized clues to vocabulary meaning and to preview the important ideas of the *Time* article. I have found that students have trouble with the level of complexity of the *Time* text, and I believe that this summary will help them to better understand it.

Activity G is used to test the students' comprehension of specific aspects of the article. Explain to the students that it is not always necessary to understand everything in an article as long as one understands enough to accomplish the purpose for reading. The purpose for reading this text is to identify cases when rules were broken by the media and to identify some of the rules that journalists try to follow.

Activities H and I are designed to help students handle the vocabulary load of the article. If they can identify the words and phrases that refer to the media, they can better sort through the details and follow the main idea of the article. Instructors need to be aware that placing the words on a continuum from general to specific is a subjective task and may spark debate among the students. Such discussion should be welcomed, and refereed, by the instructor. The answers in the teacher's manual are the author's opinion, and should be regarded as such (an opinion). The main idea of the activity is to learn to recognize synonyms and hyponyms.

Activity J gives students the opportunity to apply the rules they have discovered to other media cases.

Activities K and L are included to give the issue of media ethics a human face (lest the students begin to believe that those in the media are deliberately misusing their freedom of expression for their own gain). In this letter, the editor of *Time* explains why he chose to use the photo-illustration of O. J. Simpson on the cover. By summarizing the *who, what, when, where,* and *how* of the letter, the students will hopefully discover that thoughtful decisions can be interpreted by the public as unethical. In this world (the world of the media), much is left up to interpretation.

The journal topics (Activity M) are meant to be used to have students synthesize and apply the information presented in the chapter.

Answers

A. Sensationalism, offensive news material

B. Possible answers: Charles, the Prince of Wales; and Di, the former Princess of Wales. Though they started with a "fairy-tale" wedding, throughout the years their relationship has grown more and more strained, resulting in their divorce. Unfortunately, many think that the media helped this relationship to the grave, because it magnified each moment of the couple.

C. The issue of personal privacy and reporting. When does one forfeit one's rights to privacy? Why do we expect/allow such reporting on public figures?

D. Answers will vary.

E. Students may have underlined the following:

Paragraph 1: film; a guideline of right and wrong; allowed; by some editors; others

Paragraph 2: journalistic technique; while some think; others think; this attempt to make the quote more concise; "making up" the words; copying; have already published; many journalists feel; therefore free for others to use; plan out the picture with props and actors in order to make your story more realistic; failing to reveal that one is a reporter or actually pretending to be something else, to expose wrongdoing

1. film; 2. guideline of right and wrong; 3. techniques or ways; 4. not allowed; 5. okay, acceptable; 6. make more concise; 7. making up the words of; 8. copying; 9. free for others to use; 10. planning pictures; 11. disagreement; 12. failing to reveal one is a reporter, pretending to be something else than you are

G. *Paragraphs 1 and 2*

Media Organization	Description of What Was Done Wrong
NBC	Distorted a report about safety problems in GM trucks
USA Today	Printed a misleading picture of LA youth gang members ready to retaliate if police officers were acquitted of the Rodney King beating
Minnesota TV reporter and camera operator	Furnished alcohol to a minor to illustrate a story on teen drinking
NBC	Used footage showing fish killed during clear-cutting on government land. In reality, the forest shown was a different forest than in the story; the fish "killed" were really just stunned by researchers for testing.

Paragraphs 3–5

1. Other media outlets will be more careful not to make mistakes. They will learn from the lesson NBC had to learn the hard way.
2. Journalism as a profession has no licensing procedure, no disciplinary panels, no agreed-upon code of behavior. In other words, the rules by which the profession guides itself are unclear.
3. Reporting practices that are accepted in one news organization are forbidden in others. *Example:* going undercover to get a story about wrongdoing. Editors treat each case individually and look at all aspects in the situation before making an ethical decision.
4. Their codes of conduct are considered guidelines and are open to change as years of experience help form the code of acceptability.

Paragraphs 6–8

The Rule	*Example of How This Rule Is in Debate*
Do not falsify the facts	When a reporter makes the remarks of an interview subject more concise . . . is this fabrication? Or would the interview subject him- or herself have been more concise if he or she had written the remarks?
Do not plagiarize	Copying is wrong . . . but is using facts and quotes that another reporter has gathered without giving credit to that reporter wrong? Or are these facts and quotes now considered public domain?
Do not stage pictures	Planning a picture by the photographer is wrong . . . but what about pictures planned by the agency or group who the article is about? (UN photos, photo sessions with the president, etc.)
Do not use impersonation	TV investigative reporting uses this technique often . . . Print news considers it as lying to not identify oneself as a reporter.

H. journalists, NBC reporters, the press
General to Specific: the press, journalists, NBC reporters

I.

Paragraph	Most General ←——— to ———→ Most Specific				
1	the media	journalists		NBC	
2			—TV reporter —camera operator	—USA Today —NBC	—USA Today's Western editor —NBC News president
3	—the press —newsrooms —journalism	—reporters		—NBC	—Dateline NBC
4	—journalism —news-gathering institutions	—journalists —editors			—USA Today editor
5	—news outlets —networks			—NBC —ABC	—managers —news posts
6	—print	—journalists —reporters			
7		—news photographs —journalists	—the newspaper		—CBS's 60 Minutes
8	—network TV —print-news organizations	—reporter			—ABC's PrimeTime Live
9		—journalists		—NBC —USA Today	—Los Angeles Times managing editor

J.
1. Rights of privacy of the individual
2. The appearance of staging a photograph
3. (This one is debatable) Chung misrepresented herself as someone who could be trusted not to reveal a comment made "Just between you and me." This is not impersonation, but the concept is close.

K.

Who	—O. J. Simpson —Matt Mahurin (photo-illustrator) —managing editor of *Time* —critics of the decision
What	—a cover of *Time* magazine chosen to illustrate the fast-breaking O. J. Simpson story in June —description of the process taken and criteria used in choosing the cover —description of the controversy it caused
When	—the Saturday before the July 4 *Time* issue was to go out
Where	—Los Angeles, Chicago, New York —*Time* headquarters
Why	—to explain that the cover was not meant to be racist or to imply that O. J. was guilty —to express regret for any offense taken by any readers —to inform readers of the subjectivity involved any time that photographs are chosen to illustrate a story

L. Answers will vary. Summaries should contain (minimally) the *who, what,* and *why* information.

M. Answers will vary.

Additional/Follow-up Activities

1. Many videos are out that deal with ethical issues and the press. The following are just a start: *Absence of Malice, Broadcast News, The Paper.* Watch one of these movies as a class and have students identify the issues at work.
2. Use the Chung/Gingrich article or the O. J. Simpson article to set up a class debate over the appropriateness of the media decision.
3. Because this chapter has so many reading activities, I didn't want to include any more in the student book. However, should an instructor want to follow up on the skill of referencing, identifying the referents in the first three paragraphs of "To Our Readers" is quite challenging for students.

Chapter 3

What's News?

Opening Activity

This cartoon highlights the message of the chapter: media gatekeepers are faced with daily decisions of what to call news. The fact that media outlets are businesses as well as servants of the community sometimes creates tension for the decision makers. Have students explore these ideas by focusing on the questions.

Answers

1. A newspaper editor/publisher and a reporter
2. Many issues of great importance are in front of the editor, but the reporter wants space to print gossip. The reporter reminds the boss that gossip is what will sell papers. This is a wry comment on the tastes of the media public, as well as on the balance that an editor must try to find between being a business and a service of information for the public.
3. Possible answers include crime, political scandal, cartoons/comics, local news, and sports. The list may be as endless as the reasons why each student in a class is drawn to pick up a paper.

Objectives for Students

Content

1. Articulate criteria used by editors to select the news
2. Identify the newsworthy criteria in samples of media

3. Analyze a controversial media story in terms of its newsworthiness
4. Explain the difference between hard and soft news
5. Identify hard and soft news items

Language

Reading/Writing/Structures

Reading for a purpose; reading comprehension; guessing vocabulary in context; previewing skills; predicting skills; presenting an argument; refuting an argument; identifying techniques used in extended definitions; writing definitions; writing journal entries (in response to the ideas presented in this chapter)

Speaking/Listening

Discussing/negotiating meaning; listening for specific information; listening to an interviewed panel

Chapter Activities

I. Selecting the News

Techniques

The purpose of this section is to expose students to the criteria used by media gatekeepers in making their selection decisions concerning the news. Activities A and B are designed to have students personalize the topic by applying their own selection criteria to a set of news headlines.

Activity D focuses student attention on the use in the reading of contextualized definitions in describing assignment editors' criteria. Activity E checks student comprehension but can also be used as a springboard for a class or small group discussion about the criteria used by assignment editors. Activity F asks students to apply the concept of selection criteria. The purpose here is *not* to comprehend all of the details of each of these articles. The students should be encouraged to read for the purpose of determining what makes the article newsworthy. Once that purpose has been accomplished, the reading task can be considered a success.

Activities G and H allow students to apply the information from the text to a task. Activity G is best done in groups as it prompts much negotiation of meaning ("what do you think the article will be about, given this headline?") and decision making. Students needn't feel that there exists one right answer for this task. Though they may wish to choose the same stories as the *Lansing State Journal* did, any answer could be accepted given a convincing argument based upon the criteria stated in the text, "Decision Making in Mass Communication." The instructor may find that students are stumped as to the article content due to a lack of world knowledge or because the headline is too vague. The following synopsis of each article is provided so that the instructor is equipped to help groups determine the meaning of each headline.

1. *Chinese fakers flourish* (Bootleg U.S. goods at heart of dispute that could lead to trade war)
   Everything from CDs of American groups, to American computer components, to American liquor and medicines can be found on the streetcorners of Chinese cities . . . but these goods are not the real items, they are Chinese fakes. The trade implications of the bootleg goods have American officials concerned. Americans want Chinese officials to crack down more forcefully on such bootleg commerce.

2. *Nomination battle heats up* (White House gets more aggressive in defending surgeon general choice)
   Representatives of the White House (Vice President Gore, Mike McCurry) used stronger language attacking those who are against the nomination of Dr. Henry Foster as surgeon general. Using descriptions of "extremists" to describe right-to-life proponents, they are aggressively moving against the Republican movement to derail Foster's nomination.

3. *21 Serbs charged with atrocities* (War crimes tribunal's indictment claims rape, torture, killings in camp)
   A war crimes tribunal has charged twenty-one Serbs with committing atrocities including killing, torture, rape, and beatings against Croats and Muslims kept in a Bosnian prison camp.

4. *Dresden firebombing remembered* (After 50 years, Britons, Americans, Germans gather to heal wounds)
   On the fifty year anniversary of the Dresden firebombing of WWII, those involved commemorated the event with a time of mourning to honor those who died as a result. According to German president Roman Herzog, the gathering was held in the spirit of remembering and mourning, not revenge and hate.

5. *Investigation ends; principal to return* (But some parents not satisfied with school district's decision)
   A principal of a middle school was reinstated in his position after an

investigation found that he did no wrong. The problem began after a school game when a group of 30–40 students surrounded and threatened a car with students from another school. The principal took one student by the collar of her shirt to restrain her. She was saying that she was going to fight. A teacher thought that the principal's action was improper and filed charges against him.

6. *Law cuts drinking accidents* (MI law credited with drop in deaths but can't stop repeat offenders: Study)
A report that studied the effect of Michigan's new drunk driving laws says that lives have been saved during the last two years as a result. However, 47 percent of the drunken drivers studied had had at least one previous alcohol-related incident.

7. *Luck, legwork nab bombing suspect* (But officials believe World Trade Center case may not be closed)
The man believed to be the mastermind behind the bombing of the World Trade Center was caught after a worldwide manhunt. The United States accounts of the man's capture state that the suspect was found due to a tip from someone who lived across the street from the guesthouse in Pakistan where the suspect was found.

8. *Single and searching* (Finding romance in tri-counties a tricky, time-consuming affair)
This is an article that compares the numbers of single women to single men in different townships of the tri-county area . . . identifying places where women outnumber men and vice versa. It also suggests using some of the newer methods of meeting people: the Internet, personal ads, and dating services.

9. *Miller says petition names for bingo vote are invalid* (Democratic leaders cry partisanship at ruling by secretary of state)
The new Republican secretary of state has ruled invalid a petition to put Michigan's anti–political bingo law to a vote. The Democrats have used bingo games as a method to raise money for political campaigns. The Republicans had passed the anti–political bingo law saying that bingo was never meant to become a political fund-raising tool.

10. *Oldsmobile to put auto showroom on-line* (Lansing-based GM unit to let customers order by computer)
To help car shoppers save time and avoid haggling over prices with car salespeople, GM plans to let computer users buy cars on-line. The Internet showroom would offer one-price cars packaged with popular options. Buyers would provide a credit card number over the Net in order to put a deposit on their purchase. A local salesperson would then be notified to help finish the paperwork and provide the car!

Once students are provided with the *Lansing State Journal*'s choices for front-page coverage, the instructor can ask them to try to articulate what the *LSJ*'s news priorities are.

Activity I is a previewing activity for the following text and listening task. The first two discussion questions, "Who is Nancy Reagan?" and "What is an 'unauthorized biography?'" are designed to make sure that the students have the necessary background knowledge and vocabulary to discuss the title. The question regarding the nature of the controversy is one that encourages students to use their prediction skills. Activity J is meant to provide students with the specialized vocabulary used to describe the media actions of printing and highlighting a story. The students will need this vocabulary to adequately discuss and write about the issue at hand. Activity K is to check student comprehension of the main points of the article. However, because question #5 is critical as a backdrop for the following activities, instructors should take care to make sure students understand that the controversy isn't so much about the fact that Kitty Kelley wrote gossipy facts about Nancy Reagan as that newspapers repeated the gossip in the name of covering the release of the Kitty Kelley book.

Using the scenario discussed in "Is Gossip News?" Activities L and M further develop the controversy. To complete Activity L, students must draw upon the concept of media ethics discussed in chapter 2 and the understanding they have concerning the selection criteria that editors and publishers use in choosing the daily news coverage. I find it works well to put students into groups to generate ideas for one side of the argument or the other. If the element of competition is added (which side develops the strongest arguments or can best debate its side of the issue?), this task can generate a lot of class excitement. In addition, such discussion further develops the students' schema on the topic and prepares them to listen to the taped panel presentation.

Activity M is a challenging listening task. I would suggest first listening to the introduction of the moderator and having students identify the panelists' names and who works where. Next, play the entire tape through once, having the students identify the voice of each panelist and attempt to understand the gist of the presentation. After that, the instructor may want to play the tape over, stopping after the moderator's introduction and each panelist's contribution. Students may need to hear each panelist more than once to be able to articulate the panelist's argument.

Activity N is designed to illustrate for students the concept of counterargument and refutation. After students identify the argument to match the provided counterargument, they are encouraged to develop their own counterarguments in Activity O for the arguments presented by the media panelists in Activity M. Activity P allows students to integrate the media concepts studied thus far in chapters 2 and 3. The instructor may need to bring in more information concerning writing a persuasive essay to supply support for students who are weaker in composition skills. I use the class activity of a debate to help students generate the content of the paper and then assign the paper for homework.

Answers

A. See the synopsis of the articles in the techniques section.

B. Answers vary according to students' personal reasons.

D. 1. F;   2. B;   3. D;   4. E;   5. A;   6. H;   7. C;   8. G

E. 1. "News value" criteria encourage the coverage of sensationalistic items and discourage the coverage of news items that have a long-range impact on society.
    2. Significance, explanation and problem solving, empathy, organizational policy on certain kinds of stories, and convenience in being able to get the news

F. *Woman prepares for 120th birthday* is an example of oddity. *Parents see Ann Arbor school bias* is an example of significance—it is a problem that will likely have a long-term impact on the people of Ann Arbor. As well, it was probably covered due to the conflict expressed and the proximity of the issue to Lansing. This story most likely would not have played out of state.

G. Answers will vary.

H. The editor of the *Lansing State Journal* chose the following of the ten to be on the front page of the February 14, 1995, issue of the paper: Nomination battle heats up; Investigation ends, principal to return; Law cuts drinking accidents; Single and searching; Oldsmobile to put auto showroom on-line. Why: criteria of proximity (state government, local school issue, local industry); timeliness/empathy (single and searching . . . a way to capitalize on Valentine's Day); and conflict/explanation (surgeon general hearings).

I. Possible answers: Nancy Reagan—the wife of ex-president Ronald Reagan. Unauthorized biography—a biography printed without the request or authority of the person it is written about.

Nature of the controversy—is it ethical for newspapers to print gossip?

J. Print a story: generate press, served up, appear in newspapers, run a story

Give a story prominent coverage: Page One story, give a story front-page play, run a lead story, feature a story, run a cover story

K. 1. Kitty Kelley; 2. Nancy Reagan; 3. wrongdoing including promiscuity, child abuse, high living off taxpayer money; 4. the *New York Times, USA Today, New York Newsday, Time, Newsweek,* the *Los Angeles Times,* the *Chicago Sun-Times,* and the *Kansas City Star;* 5. Media critics wonder if the book is a valid subject for news coverage for the following reasons: Kelley uses questionable reporting methods; the book is full of hearsay and innuendo; it is a one-sided story; Kelley obviously meant to harm Mrs. Reagan's reputation with her book; it is neither a significant nor a credible work of journalism.

L. Possible answers:

Arguments for press coverage
—Nancy Reagan is a public figure; the public has a right to know about her.
—If tax money has been used improperly, the citizens should know about it.
—The issue is loaded with conflict that falls under the criterion of newsworthiness.
—The controversy surrounding the issue is newsworthy.

Arguments against press coverage
—Kelley's methods of gathering information may not be up to the ethical standards of most news organizations.
—Gossip about Nancy Reagan's private life should not be printed unless it is found to be true. (Hearsay should not be printed.)
—The biography is not significant enough to warrant national coverage.

M.

Arguments against Printing the Story		
Name of Panelist	Credentials	Argument(s)
Sheila Tate	Former press secretary for Nancy Reagan	News is supposed to be history written one day at a time. When gossip is reported by reputable news agencies, it will affect the understanding of history for generations to come. People in the future will not know it was merely gossip and will not have a standard of truth to measure it against.
Manford Bergen	Professor of journalism at University of Iowa, former editorial page editor of the *Des Moines Register*	The papers gave the story so much space that they increased the newsworthiness of the story.
David Starr	*Washington Post*	News organizations have to hold their sources of news to the same ethical standards they ask of their own reporters. Kitty Kelley is known to use second- and thirdhand accounts and rarely verifies the truth of the accounts. Printing her allegations gave them a stamp of approval.

Arguments for Printing the Story		
Name of Panelist	Credentials	Argument(s)
Carla Kandel	Spokesperson for the *New York Times*	—Story gave the public information about Nancy Reagan's influence on the presidency —Story served a local interest in New York: the publishing industry
Mara Nelson	Spokesperson for *Newsday*	—The biography may not have been newsworthy in and of itself, but the controversy it caused was newsworthy. Controversy about a public figure is newsworthy.
Michael R. McCabe	*Los Angeles Times* managing editor	—History is more than facts . . . it is the events shared by the culture. Kelley's books are events . . . Nancy Reagan is a public figure . . . Kelley made claims about both Reagans and their relationships with others that capture the readers' interest.

N. The statement best counters argument #3. The counterargument points out that it is ridiculous to use "controversy" as the criterion to justify printing a story when the act of printing the story fuels the controversy.

O. Possible answers:

Arguments against Printing the Story	
Argument(s)	Counterarguments
—News is supposed to be history written one day at a time. When gossip is reported by reputable news agencies, it will affect the understanding of history for generations to come. People in the future will not know it was merely gossip and will not have a standard of truth to measure it against.	—People in the future will be smarter than you think. They will be able to weigh the accounts of people like Kelley against those of some of the more reputable biographers. —Part of our history is the controversies of our time. The controversy surrounding this biography is worthy of historical mention.
—The papers gave the story so much space that they increased the newsworthiness of the story.	—Newspapers have limited space . . . therefore you can be sure that editors are not going to give space to any story that doesn't already have the characteristics of newsworthiness. It would be too expensive a mistake to devote space to a story that people had no interest in.
—News organizations have to hold their sources of news to the same ethical standards they ask of their own reporters. Kitty Kelley is known to use second- and thirdhand accounts and rarely verifies the truth of the accounts. Printing her allegations gave them a stamp of approval.	—If a newspaper is careful to precede Kelley's comments with "According to Kelley . . . ," the reader can discern what is the newspaper's reporting and what is Kelley's. The facts are that Kelley made certain allegations. The newspapers are objectively printing the allegations she made.

Arguments for Printing the Story	
Argument(s)	Counterarguments
—Story gave the public information about Nancy Reagan's influence on the presidency —Story served a local interest in New York: the publishing industry	—If Kelley's allegations are poorly researched they may be false. Then the information the public is getting about Nancy Reagan's influence on the presidency is false as well. The newspaper hasn't informed its audience of the truth.
—The biography may not have been newsworthy in and of itself, but the controversy it caused was newsworthy. Controversy about a public figure is newsworthy.	—It is ridiculous to use "controversy" as the criterion to justify printing a story when the act of printing the story fuels or perhaps even creates the controversy.
—History is more than facts . . . it is the events shared by the culture. Kelley's books are events . . . Nancy Reagan is a public figure . . . Kelley made claims about both Reagans and their relationships with others that capture the readers' interest.	—Hearsay should not be part of history, regardless of how much public appeal it may have. —Though public figures have their lives under the magnifying glass of the press, they have the right to have the press guarantee that the information released to the public is at least true. —Kelley's claims are suspect due to her shoddy reporting methods. She prints second- and thirdhand information and doesn't check with those actually involved to be sure the account is true. Therefore, Kelley's claims about the Reagans' relationships may not be true.

Additional/Follow-up Activities

1. Invite an editor of a local newspaper to come in and discuss issues regarding the selection of the news. What criteria does the newspaper follow? How does he or she prioritize the stories?
2. Have students analyze the content selection of the front pages of three or more different newspapers (several issues of each). Ask them to try to deduce the selection criteria and the priorities of each newspaper.
3. Have students role-play different scenarios regarding the Kitty Kelley biography. For example, Nancy Reagan runs into Kitty Kelley at a party; the *Washington Post* editor explains to Kitty Kelley why they will not print the story of the release of her book; Nancy Reagan's former press secretary goes to the *Newsday* offices to complain of their ethics in journalism, etc.

II. Hard and Soft News

Techniques

Activities A and B are meant to give students an opportunity to determine the meaning of the terms *hard news* and *soft news* from a contextualized example. Most students can extrapolate the meaning provided that they recognize that "Page One stories" refers to the Kitty Kelley press stories mentioned in the first paragraph. The definition given in Activity C allows for the students to gain an even fuller picture of the distinction between hard and soft news. Activity D is designed to have students analyze the author's definition and deduce the methods the author uses to make his definition accessible to the average reader. The accompanying language box lists some of the techniques most often used in writing extended definitions. Should the instructor want to expand on the methods of definition, an activity is provided in the teacher manual (see "Additional/Follow-up Activities"). Activity E is used to help students put names and terms to the ideas they generated in Activity D, using the information they gained from the language box. I find that the time set apart for these activities not only gives students a fuller picture of the terms *hard news* and *soft news* but also helps students better formulate their own extended definitions.

Activities F and G are created to test the students' skills at applying the previous definition. As well, doing these activities helps students to discover the sometimes fine-line distinctions between hard and soft news. It isn't always easy to decide if a news item is hard or soft, as the terms *hard* and *soft* are the extreme ends of a continuum. Sometimes a news article is balanced so carefully in the middle of the two that it is difficult to make the distinction (this issue will arise if you have students do the alternate activities). The examples given in Activities F and G are fairly straightforward, however, and shouldn't cause too much debate. However, students may struggle with the first paragraph of "NATO Official Is Questioned." Though it is true that the first paragraph is describing facts (hard news), the writer has pulled us into the story by including words such as *scandal* (appealing to those who like soft news). This is an example of how the two types of news are intertwined in much reporting. Because of the ambiguous nature of some of the decisions, it is helpful to have students work on these activities in pairs or in groups.

Activity H first can be done in small groups and then used for a classroom discussion. The concepts of media's audience and role as both a service and a business should come up in the discussion. The instructor may want students to report on the state of the news in their own countries. Is soft news as popular elsewhere as it is in the States? Do government-run news organizations resort to using soft news as a technique to boost readership? These are some of the questions that can be generated from the discussion begun in Activity H.

The journal entries in Activity I are meant to have students synthesize and personalize the concepts discussed in this chapter.

Answers

A. *Soft news:* Stories about Kitty Kelley and the publication of her new unauthorized biography of Nancy Reagan
Hard news: the recession, income taxes, the plight of postwar Iraqi refugees

B. Answers will vary, but from this example students may deduce that hard news is more serious and covers more substantial, influential topics than soft news.

D. Again, answers will vary, but students should be able to identify the form of definition, "hard news is . . . ," as well as the concrete examples that serve to give a fuller picture of the terms. They may also recognize the use of synonyms in the second and third paragraphs.

E. The author makes use of synonyms, examples, and contrast to help define hard and soft news.

F. 1. hard; 2. soft; 3. hard; 4. hard; 5. soft

G. *NATO Official Is Questioned in Belgian Case:* This article is predominantly hard news. I underlined everything from the second paragraph to the end of the article. I didn't underline the first paragraph in that I thought the author enticed us into the article using the appeal of scandal and soft news. (However, this is only my opinion.)
60 Bicyclists, Of Many Pasts: The first paragraph is hard news, the rest is soft.

H. Possible answer:

Newspapers are catering to the audience's desires and expectations for both important and interesting news. Some in the audience are only interested in the hard news regarding certain issues. These members of the audience need to see that the newspaper is committed to providing what its staff considers "serious" reporting. On the other hand, others in the audience are not drawn into reading the newspaper by seeing headlines of a serious nature. They want to be interested in something, have their attention caught by a feature article that deals with people's feelings and opinions. To market to both, newspapers are wise to include both types of articles on the front page.

I. Answers will vary.

Additional/Follow-up Activities

1. Should the instructor want to expand on the language skills presented by the language box, "Writing Extended Definitions," the following exercise may be helpful. The objective is to provide an opportunity to identify definitions using the methods described in the box. There is one best answer for each of these examples, but be aware that sometimes an author will use a combination of methods in one definition. (The answers are as follows: a. using negation; b. using examples; c. using classification; d. using comparison/contrast; e. using a synonym or words and phrases with the same meaning.)

Read the following definitions and decide which method of defining is used.

a. A *journal* is not to be confused with a magazine. A magazine has popular appeal, uses glossy paper, and is full of photographs. Generally a journal does not have a popular audience; instead it serves a special academic audience. Although a journal may have diagrams and charts to illustrate a point, it would be rare to find one with photographs.

Method of definition:

b. *Mass media* refers to methods of communication that can reach many people simultaneously and that also use some form of technology in transmitting the message. Newspapers, magazines, radio, and television are some of the most common forms of mass media.

Method of definition:

c. There are many types of *periodicals.* Newspapers are published on a daily basis, newsmagazines are published weekly, and most academic journals are distributed on a quarterly or semiannual schedule.

Method of definition:

d. Even though *constructed mediated reality* (CMR) is taken from real life, there are many differences between the two. Basically, CMR tends to be funnier, sexier, more intense, more colorful, and more violent than real life.

Method of definition:

e. *"The press"* refers to all news reporters as a collective.

Method of definition:

2. Bring several different newspapers to class: the *Wall Street Journal,* *USA Today,* the *Los Angeles Times,* and a local paper. Divide the class into small groups and have each group examine one newspaper for its coverage of hard versus soft news. What kind of coverage is predominant? Why does the group think so? Have each group present its findings and explain its conclusions to the class.

3. Have students take a survey of Americans around the campus or school. What section(s) of the newspaper do they read without fail? Which sections do they skip? Are they drawn more by the hard or the soft news of the newspaper?

4. After examining print media, bring in a national network's news report (one half hour of video). Show each story and have students decide if it is an example of hard or soft news. This can be difficult and should generate discussion and disagreement because many stories contain elements of both hard and soft news. The point is that network news has the job of reporting hard news but has to compete with sitcoms and game shows on the air at the same time, and so the network packages hard news with a lot of soft news to keep the audience from turning the channel. Hopefully students will discover this after trying (successfully or unsuccessfully) to label the TV news stories.

Chapter 4

Newspapers

Opening Activity

This activity is designed to get students to think about their own experience with one of the most accessible forms of media: the newspaper. Inherent in the answers to this question is each individual's preference for different types of news. I would do this as a small group activity because students gain a broader appreciation for the audience of newspapers in hearing what their peers expect from the newspaper.

Objectives for Students

Content

1. Identify the different eras of American newspaper journalism
2. Articulate the format and philosophy of your local newspaper
3. Name the roles and functions of the various members of a newspaper staff
4. Describe the readership of newspapers
5. Explain how the newspaper medium is responding to on-line technology

Language

Reading/Writing/Structures

Previewing text; scanning for specific information; predicting text content; reading comprehension; inferring an author's audience; determining vocabulary meaning from context; identifying patterns of textual organization; using tree diagrams; reading and visualizing statistics in graph formats; reading graphs; using graphs as source for a descriptive paragraph; bringing one's own purpose/interests to a text; inferencing; critical thinking; journal writing on the content of the chapter

Speaking/Listening

Discussing/negotiating meaning; lecture listening: getting the main idea; lecture listening: using reading text to predict the focus of a lecture; lecture listening: listening for cue words and phrases; lecture listening: listening for specific information; note-taking

Chapter Activities

I. The History of American Newspaper Journalism

Techniques

The purpose of this section is to expose students to the history and resulting trends of American journalism. Activities A and B, as well as being previewing and comprehension exercises, introduce the students to the thesis explored by the lecturer. Knowing the thesis in advance will help students to select and organize the important information in the upcoming lecture. Activity C asks the students to predict the organization and focus of the lecture, based on what they gleaned from Activities A and B. The instructor may want to go over the language box in advance of the lecture to alert students to some of the cue words and phrases that the lecturer will use to signal summary of old points and introduction of new points.

The lecture used in Activities D and E is long and full of historical details. Some background knowledge of American history will serve the students well but is not completely necessary for success. It will help the students if you divide the lecture into sections and check for comprehension before moving on to the next section. Natural places to stop the tape are after each era of journalism. You may need to play each section two or three times to assure that the students have the main ideas and the details. Students may find that the note-taking guide does not provide enough room for all of their notes. Should this be the case, recommend that they take notes on their own paper, still using the format given by the note-taking guide.

Activity F is the application activity based on the lecture. If students understand the main ideas of the lecture and have some of the supporting details, they should be able to identify each journalistic sample with its corresponding era.

Answers

B. 1. *Early:* subjective; formed in a new society; chaotic and sometimes bitter

Penny Press: objective; reflects zeal for equality and honesty in government

Yellow Journalism: subjective; sensational

Objective: objective; dispassionate attempt to report news

New: subjective; born out of the social and political changes of the 1960s; includes some bias

2. Early, Penny Press, Yellow Journalism, Objective, New

3. Each era's leaning toward objectivity or subjectivity

4. No. The clues are as follows.

Introduction: "historians differ," "the five-way division here merits some explanation," "Any division suffers from oversimplification, but this one . . ."

5. The author believes that American journalism cycles between reporting that is more objective and that which is more subjective.

C. One could expect the author to talk about each era, explain the influence of the history and the people of that era, and give examples and illustrations of the era's leaning toward objectivity or subjectivity.

D. and E.

Main Idea (Author's Thesis)			Details		
Era of Journalism	Obj. or Subj.?	Evidence for Author's Thesis	Historical Setting	Important People	Dates
Early years	Subjective	—newspapers full of opinion of whether to revolt from British —opinions found on front pages —opinions reflected those of owner/editors —advocacy reporting —early political parties sponsored papers so their ideas would be promoted	—pre-Revolution to early U.S. government: people interested in whether to revolt —after war: people interested in the form of the new government	—Benjamin Harris: first attempt to publish American newspaper —Andrew Jackson: early American president who gave *Washington Globe* a federal contract	—1690: Harris's attempt —1776: American independence from England
Penny press	Objective	—newspaper now accessible to more than the educated; common folk interested in local news (*Example: New York Sun*'s police reports) —opinion pieces separated from factual news; creation of the editorial page —birth of the wire services (AP) and the business decision to objectively cover controversial issues	—early industrial period —pre–Civil War era —social issues of time: slavery, women's rights, poverty	—Benjamin Day: produced 1 cent paper —Horace Greeley: first to create editorial page	—1833: penny paper produced by Benjamin Day

Main Idea (Author's Thesis)			Details		
Era of Journalism	Obj. or Subj.?	Evidence for Author's Thesis	Historical Setting	Important People	Dates
Yellow journalism	Subjective	—papers full of sensational stories, flashy headlines, stories about sex, scandals, and crime, pictures, color printing, and stories based on publicity stunts —stories blown out of proportion to gain more readers: Cisneros example —public opinion of Spanish/American war manipulated by press	—after Civil War to early 1900s —Spanish/American War	—Joseph Pulitzer and William Randolph Hearst (both New York newspaper owners)	—early 1900s
Objective years	Objective	—people react to excesses of yellow journalism and lean toward more objective news —publisher Adolf Ochs's success with objectivity —journalism grows as a profession; schools and standards established to uphold objectivity —media ownership changed from local owners to corporations with profit interests, not political interests	—after President McKinley's assassination	—President McKinley: his assassination blamed in part on yellow journalism's attacks —Adolf Ochs: published *New York Times* and upheld objective standards: printed speeches, etc., in entirety	—1923: establishment of American Society of Newspaper Editors standard of objectivity

Main Idea (Author's Thesis)			Details		
Era of Journalism	Obj. or Subj.?	Evidence for Author's Thesis	Historical Setting	Important People	Dates
New journalism	Subjective	—journalists' frustration with two sides to every issue —1950s, McCarthy hearings: journalists felt that facts alone don't tell the story —1958: AP and UPI began to put out more interpretive stories —1960s: journalists begin to experiment with putting their emotions into the stories	—Communist scare of the 1950s and McCarthy's hearings —1960s	—Joseph McCarthy	—1950s to now

F. *Typical Headlines:* yellow journalism; *Police Office:* penny press; *Kids Take a Pounding:* new journalism; *Worcester, May 3:* early press

Additional/Follow-up Activities

1. If students show an interest in the era of yellow journalism, you might consider showing segments of *Citizen Kane,* a thinly veiled commentary on the life of William Randolph Hearst. Sections of the movie deal with his buy-out of Pulitzer's best reporters and his pursuit of the "news."

2. Ask students to bring samples of newspaper reporting from their own countries. The class can analyze each as to its commitment to objectivity and subjectivity.

II. Exploring Your Local Newspaper

Techniques

The goal of this section is to get students into hands-on activities with their local newspapers. One objective is to have students identify what makes up their local paper. What sections does it have? Where can different types of news be found? Another purpose is to give students strategies with which to analyze the underlying philosophy of their local paper. What kind of commitment does the paper have to local news versus national and international news? Is the paper predominantly conservative or liberal—or is it neutral in its presentation of local issues?

Activities A and B are designed to show students how much information can be gained by looking only at a newspaper's content guide. In Activity A, the comparison activity allows students to see that one can determine a newspaper's audience and philosophy from the content guide alone. Activity B follows up on this, allowing students to use their critical thinking skills to predict content from the information given in the content guide.

Activity C broadens the students' search for information to what is presented on the front page. It's helpful to remind students that the front page is the newspaper's "face," what its audience will see first. The editors carefully select what goes on the front page in accordance with both their news philosophy and their audience's expectations. As the instructor, you can have students use the front page samples found in Activity C or you can bring in your own local paper and another paper for students to use. I have found that bringing in actual papers increases student motivation for the activity.

Activity D has students explore their own local paper. It is helpful to do this activity in small groups, each group having one paper to look through. Questions that ask for percentages of the paper devoted to one type of news require some sort of measuring device, like a ruler. I have students measure inches of the columns devoted to each story. This usually helps them determine the commitment to each type of news.

Activity E attempts to have students pull the information they researched into a conclusion about their paper. This may be hard for students to do without a model. I suggest that the teacher create a statement based on his or her research of a national paper. Analyzing the teacher statement in class will help students get an idea of how to do theirs. This paragraph can be given as homework for all students to complete, or you can have each group design one statement that represents the findings of its research.

Answers

A. 1. There appears to be a greater commitment to local news on the part of the *Lansing State Journal* (#2). No other content guide lists "local" as a section of the news. The *New York Times* (#3) and the *Wall Street Journal* (#1) appear to have an equal commitment to both national and international news.

2. No doubt, the *Wall Street Journal* serves the business industry. All the news is packaged in terms of the impact the event has on business.

3. Because international news begins on page A3 and national news begins on page A8, students may infer that stories on page A5 are of an international focus.

B. 1. a. the Today section; b. the Today section; c. section A, with the opinion pages and editorials; d. section A; e. section C

C. 1. The main clue to the commitment to soft news versus hard news is the information found above the title of the *Lansing State Journal.* All the blurbs are devoted to soft-type news over hard. Since the paper has given front page space to these blurbs, the intention must be to interest the audience in these feature stories. The *New York Times* gives no front page play to its soft news. This is not to say that you won't find soft news in the *New York Times.* But the paper is not marketing to the soft news reader as aggressively as the *Lansing State Journal.*

2. Definitely, the *New York Times* will provide more international coverage. Two stories of international interest are placed on the front page, while the *Lansing State Journal* is silent on international affairs. In fact, the *Lansing State Journal* doesn't present any national news items on the front page! These commitments are indicative of the different audiences of each of the papers.

D. Answers will vary according to the local newspaper analyzed.

E. Answers will vary according to the newspaper analyzed.

Additional/Follow-up Activities

1. Ask the editor of the local paper to come in and respond to the philosophy statements that the students wrote. Find out what he or she thinks about covering the different kinds of news. Ask questions regarding the particular readership of the local area. What stories would be difficult to decide to run, given this particular audience?

III. A Newspaper Staff

Techniques

Students will gain a broader picture of a newspaper staff, particularly the editorial staff, in this section. Activity A is used to draw upon the background knowledge of the students. It works well for the instructor to have the pairs report their ideas to the class. Activity B is a basic comprehension exercise. Students may need some help with the vocabulary used in describing the duties of each branch. Activities D and E work with much of the idiomatic and specialized vocabulary used in the rest of the text. Students should be encouraged to do these activities without their dictionaries, because the context clearly dictates the meanings of the words. Before going on to examine the pattern of organization used by the author, the instructor may want to make sure that students have comprehended the reading. The questions in Activity F will help to assess this.

Activities G, H, and I are designed to provide students with patterns of textual organization. If the students become familiar with such patterns, they will begin to recognize them in their outside reading. The text "Newspaper Operations and Bureaucracy" hierarchically organizes the information. I don't expect that all students will be able to complete Activity G. Its purpose is to raise student awareness to the fact that authors do use organizational modes when writing. The identification task in Activity H will further expose students to the concept of organizational strategies and provide them with visuals readers can use to organize the key points. Finally, Activity I has students go back to the text and, using the visual provided, complete the tree. I have found that the instructor is needed to guide students through Activities G and H but that Activity I can be assigned for homework.

Activities J and K allow students to apply what they have learned from the text and to check their learning. Activity J works well in small groups.

Answers

A. Answers will vary.

B. *Editorial:* to produce copy and handle the news
Advertising: to solicit and to coordinate the basic revenue-producing activities
Production: physically prints the paper, converting copy into editions
Circulation: sells and distributes the paper
Administration: handles purchasing, promotion, and accounting and coordinates the activities of the other four

D. 1. b;   2. c;   3. a;   4. c;   5. c;   6. a;   7. c;   8. b;   9. c

E. 1. E;   2. A;   3. B;   4. D;   5. C

F. 1. By putting information in declining order of significance, the editors can cut from the bottom of the story if the finished story doesn't fit into the space allotted in the paper. This keeps the writers from having to rewrite every time the story doesn't fit.

   2. The special Sunday sections of the paper hold the majority of the features or soft news. These sections include real estate, travel, television, home and garden, books, opinion, etc.

   3. City hall, the state, federal, and county governments, the courthouse and police headquarters

G. The author uses a hierarchy or classification to describe the staff of a newspaper.

H. 1. This chart would help a reader organize information from a comparison or contrast.

   2. This is a time line, used to organize the information presented chronologically by an author.

I.

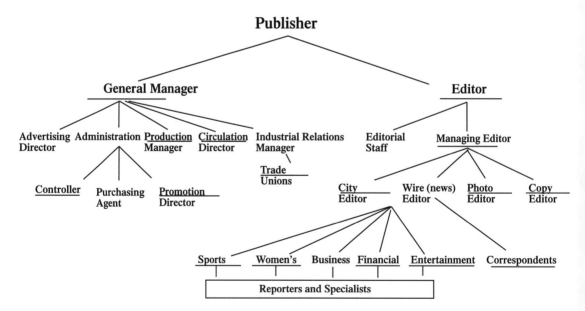

J. The first answer given is the first person in the hierarchy to contact. The positions in parentheses are those to contact should one be unhappy with the results of the first contact.

1. Advertising Director (General Manager)
2. Circulation Director (General Manager)
3. Advertising Director (General Manager)
4. Copy Editor (Managing Editor)
5. Purchasing Agent (Administration, General Manager)
6. City Editor (Managing Editor)

K. Answers will vary.

Additional/Follow-up Activities

1. A visit to your local paper is a great way to finish off this section! Most papers will give tours through every department, giving students a firsthand look at how the different positions interrelate and coordinate to produce the daily paper.

IV. Who Reads the Newspapers Anymore?

This section is designed to expose students to newspapers' audience. Activities A and B are meant to have students activate their own schema, using the audience of newspaper advertisements as a way to draw out what the students already know. Both activities work well as group work. Activity B works best if groups each have a newspaper and a pair of scissors. Actually cutting out the advertisements helps students classify them according to the sections they were found in and gives physical evidence for the conclusions.

Activity C allows students to bring their own predictions and ideas to the upcoming text, again to raise student schema. Activity E begins to help students measure their comprehension of a statistic-heavy text. However, Activities F, G, and H really help the students visualize the data by asking them to create the graphs that can be inferred from the text. I have students do Activities F, G, and H in groups. It expedites class time if each group is assigned one graph to complete in Activity H. I give each group an OHP transparency to draw their finished product on and to use in reporting to the class. (Students like this activity because it is like a puzzle for them; they have to search the text for the relevant information and represent the information visually.)

Activity I asks students to compile all the information discussed and make conclusions based upon the findings. This often works best as homework. Activity J asks students to infer even more from the text. I explain it to my students this way: "The text is written from a set of graphs and data. But the set of graphs and data was collected first by use of a survey. Try to reconstruct the survey using the information given in the text." Partners or groups can work on this task, or it can be given as homework.

Answers

A. 1. *Wallpapers to go:* late 20s on up; male or female but more likely female; have expendable income but not super rich; homeowners
A Midwinter's Tale: 25+; well educated; have expendable income; like to read and watch plays; go out to the shows
Golfers: 22+; male and female but more likely male; expendable income; like sports (especially golf!)
Menopause: 45+ (perhaps younger if a family member is currently going through menopause); female; all incomes

    2. *Wallpapers to go:* women's, home, or lifestyle section; perhaps local or national news section
A Midwinter's Tale: entertainment section
Golfers: sports section
Menopause: women's section

B. 1. Answers will vary.
    2. Answers will vary.
    3. Most newspaper advertising is aimed at adults as opposed to teens or children.

C. 1. Answers will vary.
    2. Possible answers: businesspeople; politicians; those with careers established; students with an interest in current events, etc.
    3. Possible answers: young people heavily involved in school or outside events; the uneducated, etc. (these answers aren't necessarily right, but students could make a case supporting these ideas)

E. 1. T; 2. F; 3. F; 4. T; 5. T; 6. F; 7. F; 8. F

F. Age; Marriage and family status; Gender; Political affiliation; Education level

G.

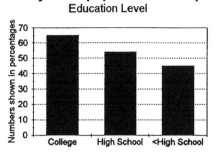

Daily Newspaper Readership
Education Level

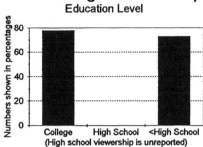

TV News Program Viewership
Education Level
(High school viewership is unreported)

H.

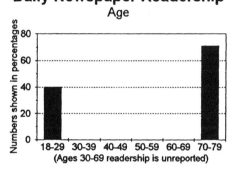

Daily Newspaper Readership
Age
(Ages 30-69 readership is unreported)

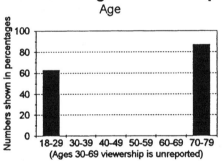

TV News Program Viewership
Age
(Ages 30-69 viewership is unreported)

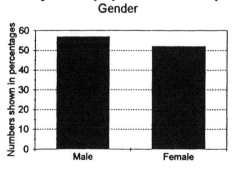

Daily Newspaper Readership
Gender

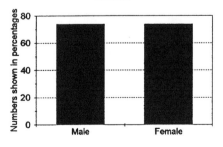

TV News Program Viewership
Gender

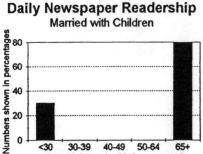

Daily Newspaper Readership
Married with Children

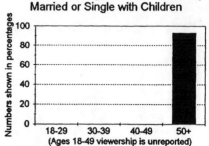

TV News Program Viewership
Married or Single with Children

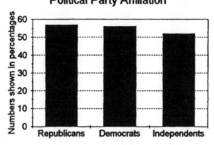

Daily Newspaper Readership
Political Party Affiliation

I. Answers will vary.

J. The survey may have looked something like this.

Personal Data

Age: _____

Sex: _____ Male _____ Female

Status: _____ Married _____ Single _____ Children

Political Party: _____

Education Level: (check highest you have received)

_____ No high school diploma _____ High school graduate

_____ College graduate

Media Usage

1. Do you read a daily newspaper? _____ Yes _____ No
2. Did you read a newspaper yesterday? _____ Yes _____ No
3. Do you watch a TV news program regularly? _____ Yes _____ No

(4.)   Did you watch a TV news program   _____ Yes   _____ No
       yesterday?

(#4 is not stated in the article, but some students may infer that it was asked but that Debra Gersh did not report it.)

Additional/Follow-up Activities

1. Using the reconstructed survey in Activity J, have students conduct their own poll to see if they get similar results. Perhaps have students go further and ask survey participants several *why*-type questions.
2. Ask the advertising director of a local newspaper to come to describe the paper's readership.

V. Newspapers in the Future

This section is meant to expose students to the current trends in newspaper publishing, especially the advent of on-line publishing. Because this is a new trend and all the implications have not yet been discovered, let alone worked out, nobody knows where it will lead and what it will someday mean for traditional newspapers. Hopefully students will finish this section with an understanding of some of the implications and an interest in following the field as it develops.

Activity A is designed to activate student schema regarding the issue and place the students in the position of the decision makers in the newspaper industry who must try to respond to a declining audience and the new technologies available. This activity works best in small groups, because more ideas are generated. The instructor can have each group present its ideas to the class.

Activity B has students use previewing skills to help them heighten their schema toward the content of the article. The instructor should stress that all the questions can be answered from the headlines and visuals. A careful reading of the article is not needed to complete this task. Activity C further prepares students for the article by having them deal with the vocabulary present in the article. I recommend doing this activity before having students read the article.

Activity E serves as a comprehension task to see if students can find advantages of on-line publishing other than the ones highlighted in the headlines. Activity F asks students to go beyond the text to try to understand the viewpoint of a person interviewed for the article. To answer this, they will need to assess the value of print newspapers in history, the present, and the future.

Activity G, the journal questions, is designed to help students synthesize and personalize the information covered in the chapter.

Answers

A. No answer is "wrong" in this activity. Possible answers include developing a section for the issues and concerns of the younger generation,
adding more color to attract an audience, and going on-line themselves.

B. 1. Fifty-one
2. Up-to-date information, no advertisements, and (inferred) no ink or
paper costs
3. America Online, Prodigy, Compuserve, Delphi, Ziff Davis
Interchange

C. The answers given are those that can be inferred from the context.

1. *electronic publishing:* sending articles to readers over the Internet,
local dial-up services and online services
online services: a computer service
2. *went on strike:* stopped working
3. *World Wide Web:* an international information service
4. *surcharge:* a cost paid for by the consumer
5. *posted:* put on the computer; printed
6. *breaking news:* updates to the news, mostly coming from the wire
services.
7. *death sentence:* a prediction of death
endure: last; continue

E. Allows for publishing to continue during times of labor strikes; hourly
or minute-by-minute updates of breaking news; money saved on
distribution costs; allows for electronic searches of back issues of the
paper; increases the (local or school) newspaper's readership to people
from around the world; technology and system for on-line publishing
are inexpensive and require little maintenance

F. Possible answers:
Though the technology for newspapers may be inexpensive, the majority of homes do not yet have computers with on-line access; people like
to carry and read the news while commuting to work . . . it would be
harder to do this with on-line newspapers; people often buy newspapers
for local advertising, which would be eliminated with on-line
publishing.

G. Answers will vary.

Additional/Follow-up Activities

1. Have students conduct a poll to find out where most people they know get their news. Ask what attracts each person to that form of the news.
2. If you have the technology available, have students cruise the Internet to find some of the newspapers that are publishing on-line. Ask students to report on their findings and discuss what they thought of the experience of reading the news on-line.

Chapter 5

Radio

Opening Activity

This activity is meant to direct student attention to radio as a medium, and consider the specialized audiences that radio maintains. To conduct this activity, tape no more than one minute of a rock and roll song and play it for the class.

Answers

This is a rock and roll station. The audience would be primarily younger: teens through the twenties.

Objectives for Students

Content

1. Describe the "golden age" of radio
2. Identify two aspects of a successful radio play
3. Identify modern program formats of radio
4. Explain how radio has maintained a position of influence in the world of media
5. Discuss the phenomenon of "talk radio" and its impact on today's society

Language

Reading/Writing/Structures

Identifying the main idea; identifying supporting detail; outlining as an organizational tool; predicting text content; determining vocabulary meaning from context; applying textual information to a task; using cohesive devices; comprehending text; previewing; writing a "formula" story; reading and interpreting charts and graphs; inferencing; thinking critically; writing journal entries in response to the content of the chapter

Speaking/Listening

Discussing/negotiating meaning; predicting; listening to a radio play; describing a chart or a graph; making a presentation with visual support; listening to modern radio programming; listening to an interview; describing another person's point of view

Chapter Activities

I. The Golden Age of Radio

Techniques

This section sets up the historical setting of the medium of radio. It is designed to expose students to radio's heyday, commonly known as the "golden age" of radio. Knowing the history of radio programming prepares students to analyze the current trends in radio and also to understand the early programming trends of television (chap. 6).

Activity A is used to activate student schema toward the topic of radio programming. Since most students are not familiar with early American trends, it works well to find out how radio grew and developed internationally. I conduct this activity as a class discussion. Students find that their cultural differences extend to the types of radio programming available.

The text in Activity B is a basic history of early American radio. Activities C, D, and E are designed to have students interact with the main ideas and details of the text and, therefore, comprehend it more completely. Activity C can be done in pairs or small groups. The titles that students generate should indicate the main idea of each section. Activity D exposes students to an outline that is nearly complete. The purpose is to provide a model of an outline so that students can better complete Activity E. I find it helpful to do Activity D in class and then ask students to complete Activity

E for homework. Activity E can also be done in small groups, but it works better if you divide up the workload between the groups (e.g., assign each group to complete a different section of the outline).

Activities F through I are included to give students a taste of some of the elements that made radio during this era so successful. Activities F and G have students work with the sound effects that so characterized the radio dramas of the golden age. Activity F is used as a model of the use of sound in radio drama. Activity G provides students with the opportunity to become sound technicians themselves. Activities H and I introduce students to the demands placed on the writers of the early radio dramas and provide students with the strategy employed by the head writer of *The Lone Ranger*: developing and using a formula to generate stories. Activity H asks students to identify the "bad guys" discussed in the formula. This activity is to help students with the literary vocabulary presented in the formula (i.e., antagonist). Activity I has students use the formula given by Mr. Striker to write their own stories. I have often given this activity for homework. However, if the instructor has the class time available, it is fun to have students collaborate on the finished product. Here is one method of doing so. Have students sit in a circle. Under a time limit, each student begins by writing step one of the formula. Students then pass their writing to the person to their right and are given a new time limit to read their classmate's beginning and to add step two of the formula to the story. The process continues until the formula has been completed. Either way, writing at home or in class as a group, students enjoy the opportunity to write creatively.

Answers

A. Answers vary from country to country.

C. 1. *Paragraphs 1–3:* Radio's early uses and history
2. *Paragraphs 4–6:* Radio as a source of entertainment
3. *Paragraphs 7–8:* Radio as a source of news and information
4. *Paragraph 9:* Radio after the "golden age"

D. I. Historical background of radio broadcasting
  A. Radio as a communication tool
    1. *Ship-to-ship, ship-to-shore communication*
      a. Used during sea emergencies
        i. Ex: The Titanic in 1912
    2. Military, police, and pilot communication
  B. Radio as a broadcasting tool
    1. Experiments began approximately 1910

a.   *Lee De Forest's Metropolitan Opera House broadcast*
2.   Broadcasting possibilities envisioned
   a.   Public informed quickly
   b.   Public has option other than print media
C.   RCA's role
   1.   Radio sales boom
      a.   1925—in 10% of all homes
      b.   *1930—in 46% of all homes*
   2.   Sarnoff's idea
      a.   Idea proposed to maintain radio sales
      b.   Create entertainment programming organization
   3.   NBC formed by RCA

E.   Students may use their own words and phrases to complete this task. The following is one possible answer.

II.   Radio as a source of entertainment
   A.   *Music entertainment*
      1.   Symphony
      2.   *Big Band*
         a.   *Tommy Dorsey*
         b.   *Duke Ellington*
         c.   *Benny Goodman*
         d.   Glenn Miller
   B.   Comedy programming
      1.   *Amos 'n' Andy*
         a.   *about a group of black workers*
         b.   *aired each weekday from 7:00–7:15 P.M. through the 1930s*
         c.   *very popular*
            i.   *movie theaters would stop films to broadcast Amos 'n' Andy*
            ii.   *restaurants and stores would broadcast program*
         d.   white actors and actresses
         e.   *played on racial stereotypes for humor*
   C.   *Soap opera programming*
      1.   *The Guiding Light*
      2.   *Our Gal Sunday*
   D.   *Action-adventure dramas*
      1.   *The Shadow*
      2.   *The Green Hornet*

      3. *The Lone Ranger*
III. *Radio as a source of news and information*
   A. Wartime news
   B. *Roosevelt's fireside chats*
IV. Radio's role after the "golden age"
   A. *Television took over role of entertainment programming*
   B. *Radio remained strong communication medium*
      1. *Growth of music industry*
      2. *Development of talk and news programming*

F.

CHICAGO MORNING

It was a cold winter morning in Chicago. Paul was sound asleep in his warm bed. Outside the strong northeast wind blew (*) across the lake, and the window shutters beat rhythmically (*) against the house. Suddenly, the radio alarm went off (*). From a distant room, the phone rang (*). Sleepy Paul sat up quickly in bed, yawned (*), and stretched. Then he jumped up, and hit the radio alarm clock (*). He looked out the windows and heard a train (*) and, in the distance, the sound of a fire engine bell (*). Again the phone rang (*), and he stumbled across the room, bumping his leg on the bed as he went (*) and scaring his dog (*). He picked up the phone and said "Hello" (*). But no one answered. All he heard was a low and dull dial tone (*). Paul slammed down the phone (*) and prepared himself for another day in the city.

H. Villain, antagonist, crooks

I. Stories will vary.

Additional/Follow-up Activities

1. Ask an American over age 55 to come in and be interviewed about the experience of having the radio be his or her source of entertainment. Have students prepare questions beforehand to make sure the conversation is rich with information. Find out this person's view of early radio programming versus that of today.
2. Bring in samples of old-time radio broadcasts for students to listen to.
3. Have groups write a radio play complete with sound effects based on the stories produced from Activity I.

II. Modern Radio Formats

This section is included to answer the question of what has happened to radio since television has taken over the role of family entertainment. How has radio managed to maintain a hold on the media market? And what can we expect to find in terms of programming around the radio dial? Activity A asks students to draw on their own experience to brainstorm an answer to the first question. Then the text selection for Activities B through F, "Playing the Quick Change Game," provides some of the industry's answers to that same question. Activity B is a previewing activity, again showing students that with a careful preview (in this case, reading the title and the first paragraph), one can accurately predict the content and focus of an article. Activity D asks students to examine the text for its clues to the descriptions of each type of radio format. Activity E has students take what they have gleaned from the article and apply that information to a broader task of matching descriptions to each radio format listed. It works well to put students in pairs to work together on both Activities D and E. Activity F provides an opportunity to check overall comprehension of the text.

The materials in Activities G through J present students with an answer to the second question: What can we expect to find on the radio in terms of modern programming? The charts and graphs indicate the changes in programming formats in the past ten years. The purpose of the project outlined in Activities G through J is to provide a natural context in which students will study and apply the information found in the charts and graphs. I find this project to work best in small groups, and if groups are assigned, teachers should specify that the final presentation (Activity K) must use each member of the group as a speaking participant.

Activity G sets up the task by giving the broad goal and then asking students to complete the steps necessary to accomplish the goal. The broad goal is to choose a radio program format (country, classical, contemporary hit, etc.) that will draw the largest audience in Alaska. It may help to outline the steps to the students before they begin the task.

1. Step one in choosing a radio format is to describe one's audience. The chart and graph in Activity G provide students with some of the demographic information they will need to describe their audience.
2. Step two is to examine the programming trends in the radio industry over a period of time. The charts and graphs given in Activity H provide such information.
3. Step three is to make predictions of which formats will be most successful. Students will need to extrapolate these predictions from the charts and graphs given in Activity H.

4. Step four is to find out what programming already exists in the Alaskan radio market. The table provided in Activity H gives the students this information.
5. Step five is to take all the information determined in steps one through four and make a decision of what radio programming format students will offer.

In Activity I, students are asked to present their conclusion and articulate the information that was critical in making that decision. Students will need to select the information they used from the charts and graphs that helped them to make their decision. Activity J prepares students for the final presentation by giving students a format for presenting information from a chart or graph. I find it helps to first model the task for the whole class and then have pairs practice describing a given chart or graph to each other. Activity K is the actual presentation. Usually groups need some class time to organize their presentation beforehand.

Activity L introduces students to three different radio formats and asks students to try to identify each format throughout all the programming offered by a station. This is a fun activity and can be conducted as a whole class activity. Activity M follows up on Activity L. It encourages students to extrapolate from their experience in completing Activity L.

Answers

A. Possible answers include the development of the music industry, the fact that radio can be used while doing something else (it doesn't require rapt attention), the decision to include radios as a basic car feature, etc.

B. 1. Radio has the ability to adjust or change according to changes in public taste. Radio has changed quickly as needed to maintain its audience.
2. Its ability to adapt quickly

D.

Name of Format	Description of Format
Album-Oriented Rock (AOR)	—once popular, now making a comeback.
Contemporary Hit Radio (CHR)	—list of top songs shorter than was typical in the 1970s; accompanied by humorous deejay banter —dominates airwaves
Adult Contemporary Hit Radio	—a subgenre of CHR
Eclectic-Oriented Rock (EOR)	—(not defined in the text)
Golden Oldies	—appeals to children of the sixties
Fifties Rock (nostalgia radio)	—dropping in popularity
Talk	—found mostly on AM stations, cheaper to buy syndicated or network-originated than to produce own
Children's	—aimed at young children and their mothers

E. 1. e; 2. c; 3. g; 4. f; 5. a; 6. b; 7. d

F. 1. The fragmenting of established formats into tinier pieces; the emergence of new formats and programming; efforts to recruit specific listeners
2. The number of stations offering "golden oldies," a format that appeals to the Yuppie audience, is up.
3. The younger audience is turning to music-video services like MTV to hear their music.

G. A sample summary may be like this.

Of the approximately 400,000 people living in Alaska, the predominant age range is from 25–44, accounting for over 50% of the population. There are more men than women represented in every age range reported. Nearly one-half of the population is involved in government and service jobs. Retail makes up 18% of the workforce, and labor-type jobs account for approximately 23% of the workforce.

H. Trends that students may notice in helping them make their decision. From the graphs

1. The country format holds a large percentage of the market and has increased its influence in the eight years reported.
2. News/talk has more than doubled its influence in the last eight years.
3. Adult CHR, as well as variety, has lost some of its audience in the years reported.

From the Alaskan Formats table

4. Knowing that adult and variety are losing their audience and that they already represent a large percentage of the Alaskan formats, students would not be wise to choose one of these. Knowing that country and news/talk are increasing in the trends reported, it may be wise to create a new station with one of these formats, depending on what is already in the local area.

Students may choose any format, as long as they can justify their choice. I would choose country, given its larger market. But someone could argue that AOR is making a comeback and is not well represented in the Alaskan market. Any choice, given a good argument, can be accepted. The key is to see that students are interpreting the information in the graphs correctly and are making logical conclusions.

I. Student projects will vary.

J. Here is a model of one description based on the graph titled "U.S. Radio Formats"

1. This is a graph detailing the format programming trends in the United States in the years 1986, 1990, and 1994. It indicates the numbers of stations playing each format and shows whether formats are increasing or decreasing in numbers nationwide.
2. The graph is a bar chart using different colors to differentiate the data of each year.
3. I will present the data pictured from left to right.

4. I will focus on the categories of country, adult, news/talk, and AOR, because they are the formats our group has considered for adoption.

5. As you can see, the country format dominates the market and is increasing in its influence. Whereas, though the adult format is also a dominant force, it is decreasing in numbers nationwide.

6. As a result, we believe that country will take some of the adult audience in the future.

L.

	Country	*AOR*	*Fine Arts*
News	B	A	C
Advertising	C	B	A
Deejay banter	C	A	B
Weather	A	B	C

M. 1. News and weather are least likely to reflect the program format.
2. Possible answers: people expect their news and weather to have a professional, objective tone; the objective content of news and weather make it harder to change how they are packaged

Additional/Follow-up Activities

1. Take a poll of teenagers' radio listening habits to find out if they really prefer MTV over the radio.
2. Have students take a "survey" of the area radio stations. What formats are available on what stations? How much of the programming is devoted to music, ads, info/news, etc.? Have students listen for an evening and come back with conclusions.
3. Take students to a local radio station. Find out how the station knows how many people are listening to its programming, how the station identifies its audience, and how the overall programming schedule is packaged.
4. If a trip is not possible, invite a representative from a local station to speak to the class and answer any questions they may have.

III. An Influential Format: Talk Radio

Techniques

This section examines a popular radio format: talk radio. Students are exposed to the concept of talk radio and then introduced to one talk show host in particular: Rush Limbaugh.

Activities A, B, and C serve to add to students' background information about talk radio. Activity A is an introduction to the concept of talk radio. Students examine their own experiences and ideas concerning talk radio before reading the selection. Activity C asks students to use the article to add to their own ideas already identified in Activity A.

Activities D through H are designed to build student schema concerning Rush Limbaugh. (Many students have never heard of him and have no knowledge base to bring to the article "What a Rush!") By examining the opinions expressed in Activities D through H, students begin to understand how controversial Rush is. They also begin to formulate ideas concerning who is likely to like Rush and who is likely to dislike him. Activity D asks students to determine the opinion of the car owner whose bumper sticker proclaims, "Flush Rush." This should be apparent to students, provided they know the meaning of "flush." Activities E, F, and G require the student to identify the opinions stated in the letter, both for and against Rush Limbaugh. The NOW letter is decidedly negative on Rush; however, the letter repeats others' more positive comments on Rush. The letter can be read for homework, but Activities F and G are interesting to discuss in class.

Activities H and I are previewing tasks. In Activity H, students are to relate the information they find to the NOW letter. Activity I asks students to use their prediction skills. Activity J deals with descriptive sentences found in "What a Rush!" Students use the main ideas and identify the supporting details of each. Because this is done before reading, the task of comprehending the article becomes easier for the students. This activity can be done individually or in pairs.

Activities L and M continue to provide language support for the article "What a Rush!" Activity L is a vocabulary in context exercise. Pairs or groups of students should be encouraged to make guesses of words that could fit into the place of the blank spaces. Once the students have made their own guesses, the instructor can put up the real words on the OHP (not in order). Students can then try to match their guesses with the words they know. Activity M asks students to identify the missing main ideas or supporting details, using the text as their guide. This can be conducted as an individual activity or can be done in pairs if students seem intimidated by the reading.

Activity N is a listening activity based on people's opinions of Limbaugh. Activity O requires that students have comprehended and synthesized the information in Activity N. These can be conducted as a jigsaw activity if desired by the instructor.

Activity P provides students an opportunity to synthesize and personalize the issues and information discussed in the chapter.

Answers

A. 1. Answers will vary.
2. Answers will vary.
3. Possible answers: to feel a part of the larger society; to pass time while driving; to lessen feelings of loneliness; to feel empowered by hearing your point of view expressed; to feel empowered by hearing other's problems ("At least I'm not that bad!"); etc.
4. Possible answers: to engender a community attitude; to promote a societal value; to inform the populace; etc.

C. To be added to question 3: a medium for broadcasting one's ideas and opinions; to promote an organization's public relations and ideas; to provide companionship and company; to provide contact with people

D. "Flush Rush" indicates that the owner of the car would equate Rush and his ideas with that which should be disposed of down a toilet. The owner is against Rush and his ideas.

F. 1. The National Organization for Women
2. Most likely, women (and men) who support the agenda of women's rights (including abortion rights). Reading deeper, this letter was probably sent to Democrats rather than to Republicans.
3. Abortion rights advocates, Democrats, women's rights advocates, liberals, progressives
4. Pro-life advocates, Republicans, conservatives

G. Most dangerous man in America; doing good work; hateful, divisive fanatic; intolerant; bigoted; humorous; clever; a harmless little fuzzball

H. American original; hard-edged humor; hard-right views; funny; "right"

I. Possible answers: The article introduces basic information about Rush Limbaugh and his rise in influence both politically and socially; however, the article appears to deal predominantly with his political influence.

J. 1. 2;   2. 1;   3. 2;   4. 1;   5. 1;   6. 2;   7. 2;   8. 1;   9. 2

L. 1. constituents;   2. switchboard;   3. monitoring;   4. rivals;
5. blossoming;   6. sufficient;   7. tuned him in;   8. infested;
9. disingenuous;   10. operatives

M.

Paragraph	Main Idea	Supporting Idea
5	A description of the type of person who listens to talk radio	—conservatives who believe media has a liberal bias
		—4 out of 10 Americans
		—Republican and conservative
		—those who feel left out of the loop
6 and 7	Limbaugh is closely linked to Republican Party.	—He did fund-raisers for Republican candidates.
		—He was greeted like a hero at the GOP convention.
		—Republican National Committee bought commercial time on his show to oppose a Clinton economic package.
		—He stays in contact with key Republican politicians and promotes party ideas on his show.
		—Newt Gingrich concedes there is a "close symbiotic relationship" between party leaders and Limbaugh.

N.

	Person 1	Person 2	Person 3	Person 4
What is your opinion of Rush Limbaugh?	Can't stand him, hates watching/ listening to show. Has to leave room when show is on.	He's an outspoken man who is sometimes taken out of context by those who don't listen to him much. Takes him with a grain of salt, finds him to be an alternative news source. Gets tired of his flamboyancy.	Not a fan of his. He is good at what he does, but he doesn't accurately reflect the truth.	He's not that bad! He's entertaining, has funny "in your face"– type songs, etc.

	Person 1	Person 2	Person 3	Person 4
Which of his ideas do you agree with?	Little details of some of his arguments	The government has gotten too large; people should be taking more responsibility for their actions and should take care of fellow community members rather than expecting the government to come in and handle the problems. We need a balanced budget; it will require hard choices. Limiting the regulations of government.	His criticism of how much money Congress spends. His comments on the extremes that liberals will go to to promote their causes.	That network media is on the liberal side and is biased against conservatives
Which of his ideas do you disagree with?	His view of economics and politics (e.g., the idea that anyone who works hard enough can achieve the American dream)	His ideas on the environment: clearcutting and endangered species	His view of those who haven't made it in America. His connections with big business and conservatives in politics.	His stance on the environment. Doesn't recognize the looming crisis in the environment.

	Person 1	Person 2	Person 3	Person 4
How has Rush impacted American politics?	He encourages conservative white people to justify their ideas/ viewpoints and motivates them to vote and call their politicians to express their views.	He has emboldened a group of people who might have felt that no one was speaking up for them. He's made people question more of what they hear from the government.	The 1994 election that brought conservatives into a majority position in government was influenced by him.	He's Republican; perhaps the 1994 elections were influenced . . . but maybe people would have voted that way anyway. Gives good arguments for conservatives to use in discussions with friends.
How has Rush influenced American society in general?	Probably not much . . . perhaps by making the radio call-in show a popular forum for people.	The phenomenon of the "dittoheads" and those who get their kicks out of bashing him. Making people question the news they hear.	He has contributed to the lack of civility in public discourse. He's made it acceptable to be abrasive to those who don't agree with one's opinion.	The popularity of talk radio was helped along by people like Rush.

O. 1. Person 4 has the best opinion of Rush Limbaugh. Person 2 is somewhat positive.
2. Person 1 probably thinks the least of Rush. Person 3 also thinks little of Rush but is not so vocal in his displeasure.
3. Rush's ideas of the economy . . . that anyone in America can be successful if he or she works hard enough. Rush's stance on environmental issues.

P. Answers will vary.

Additional/Follow-up Activities

1. Bring in listening passages from different types of talk radio to show the range of what is available. Example: Larry King, Dr. Ruth, etc. Discuss issues of purpose (entertainment, information dissemination, political clout).

2. Show the movie *Talk Radio* and discuss the issues it covers.

3. As further introduction to the Limbaugh article: Bring in a video segment of his TV show. Show only enough for students to be able to answer the following: (1) What adjectives can be used in describing the personality of Rush Limbaugh? (2) What kind of people would find Rush amusing or informative? (3) What kind of people would not find Rush amusing or informative?

4. *Frontline* has produced a show about Rush Limbaugh called "Rush Limbaugh's America." It is possible that the media center of your local or school library has access to this video. If not, it can be obtained by writing or calling

PBS Video
1320 Braddock Place
Alexandria, VA 22314
1-(800) 328-PBS1

Chapter 6

Television

Opening Activity

The cartoon selected for the opening activity draws student attention to the role that television plays in our lives. Most of us would say that we use television as an information or entertainment source. However, this cartoon alludes to the subconscious needs that television fulfills. As students discuss the cartoon, any interpretation can be accepted as long as it helps to turn student attention to television and its role in their own lives.

Answers

1. Possible answer: Calvin is hoping for some sympathy from the teacher and some sort of acknowledgment of his learning style. Instead, she ignores his comment, making him realize that the only place he has his learning style fulfilled is in front of a television.
2. It provides information in the small pieces (factoids) that he can take in.
3. Possible answers: He may be saying that television viewing has shortened the attention span of children. He may be saying that the education system is inflexible in adjusting to the changes in children. (Let the reader form his or her own interpretation!)

Objectives for Students

Content

1. Discuss the types of programming available on television
2. Identify the traditional programming time slots

3. Present evidence of the predominance of television in today's society
4. Discuss the impact of television on education
5. Discuss television's role in reflecting/promoting societal stereotypes
6. Discuss the relationship between television and violence in society

Language

Reading/Writing/Structures

Comprehending academic text; applying textual information to a task; reading and interpreting graphs; scanning for specific information; reading critically; identifying an author's audience and purpose; identifying an author's attitude toward a topic; identifying supporting details of main ideas; using referencing skills; determining vocabulary from context; developing research skills; writing a letter of opinion; evaluating a source of information; thinking critically; writing journal entries in response to the content of the chapter

Speaking/Listening

Discussing/negotiating meaning; listening to a conversation; listening to a lecture; listening for facts and statistics; expressing an opinion; using facts in counterarguments; debating an issue

Chapter Activities

I. Television Programming

Techniques

This section is to provide students with a brief historical context of television programming and then focus on the current programming genres and trends. Activities A, B, C, and D set the historical context and inform students that television inherited most of its early programming ideas from radio. Activity A is to be conducted as a class discussion. The instructor may have groups role-play the interaction between the person from the past and a modern television viewer. Activity B requires that students apply the information they learned in the previous chapter. Activity D provides a comprehension check for the text given in Activity C.

Activities E and F serve as an introduction to the types (or genres) of television programming available. Activity E asks students to identify their personal preference in programming (given a choice of three shows). Activity F has students listen to a three-way conversation between friends discussing their likes and dislikes in television programming. Both activities set the schema for the text in Activity G.

Activities H and I are meant to give students a chance to reflect on their own experiences with television programming. Often the kinds of programming and the scheduling of that programming will differ from country to country. This discussion task leads nicely into the text given in Activity J. Though the text describes American programming, the instructor can continue the crosscultural comparison by encouraging students to think about how these programming time periods are used in their own countries. Activity J can be done as a class or assigned for homework.

Activity K works well as a group activity. The purpose of the activity is to have students use what they have learned about programming genres and scheduling to help them decide on the appropriate time slots for each program.

Answers

A. 1. This is an amusing statement in that television has become such a dominant force in broadcasting. In fact, the average American family has found much time for television in its life.

2. Possible answers: you could tell the author of the statement about the popularity of television, the "couch potato" phenomenon, the fact that television has become a common denominator in informing the country of the pop culture events (the Olympics, who shot J. R., etc.).

B. Music programming, drama and comedy, soap operas, action-adventure programs, informative programming

1. Possible answers: Music and informative programming. These are most easily listened to while doing something else. Any type of programming that requires one to sit down and pay attention would be better on television.

2. Entertainment programming, like soap operas, action-adventure, drama

D. 1. Television's program content came from radio programming: the first hit television shows were radio successes transposed to television, and many famous television stars were first radio personalities. Also, television borrowed the economic system of radio and thus developed much faster.

2. Both television and newspapers were first available in public places before they gained popularity in individual households.

3. Because television was at that time viewed in local bars and taverns (inferred: and drew a primarily adult male audience) and because of the visualness of television which makes sense in sports programming
4. Once television became a household item, the audience became more diverse and included women and children. Thus, television began to program to meet the needs of this more diverse population.

E. Answers will vary.

F. 1. Pat, 2; Bryan, 3; Carol, 1
  2. *Pat:* realistic, engaging, deals with current issues, developed characters, makes her think
  Carol: don't make me think, entertain me! shows that are relaxing
  Bryan: educational, true reality programming, informing

G. *Pat:* medical drama; *Carol:* sitcom; *Bryan:* nature

H. Answers will vary.

I. Answers will vary.

J. 1. *Prime time* programming is from 8 to 11:00 P.M. EST and is filled with network programming. Little programming is done "live" except for certain news and sports programming. Some shows are filmed in front of a live audience. Genres found during prime time: action-adventure series, sitcoms, movies, specials, and miniseries.
  Weekday daytime programming is from 7:00 A.M. to 5:00 P.M. Genres found: quiz and game shows, soap operas, reruns of network series, and news shows like *Good Morning America.*
  Weekend daytime is from 7:00 A.M. to 5:00 P.M. on Saturday and Sunday. Genres found: Saturday: children's programming and sports; Sunday: network news, public affairs shows, and religious programming.
  Fringe time is from 5:00 to 8:00 P.M. and 11:00 P.M. to 1:00 A.M. Genres of programming found: news, syndicated programs, talk shows, and movies.
  2. Local stations have started soaps earlier and scheduled game shows to lead into the local news. Network affiliates have pressed to have prime time start earlier, at 7:00 P.M.

K. Answers will vary, but these guidelines should be followed.

> *Gum Drop Safari:* most likely scheduled for Saturday mornings or weekday daytime
>
> *Yours for the Taking:* most likely scheduled weekday daytime or fringe time
>
> *Life and Death:* prime time, later in the evening due to adult and disturbing content
>
> *Audrey:* fringe time or weekday daytime
>
> *Weekly Views with Big Shots:* Sunday daytime
>
> *Cheers:* fringe time
>
> *Time Divine:* Sunday daytime
>
> *Room One:* prime time

Additional/Follow-up Activities

1. Have students conduct their own research about the types of programming found on one station over the course of 24 hours (or a week).
2. Bring in videotaped examples of the most commonly found genres of programming. Have students try to identify the type of programming after watching only 3–5 minutes of each program.
3. Take an informal class poll to find out the most popular types of programming among the class members. Ask each student to explain why he or she prefers one type of programming over another.

II. The Predominance of Television

Techniques

This section is designed to provide students with the facts and statistics that indicate the overwhelming impact television has made in the lives of Americans. Activity A activates student schema by asking them to bring their world knowledge and personal opinions to the issue and make guesses as to if each real statistic is higher or lower than the one stated. Activity B follows up on the same statements and has students listen for the true figures from a lecture. This lecture-listening activity is somewhat challenging for students because they are listening for details as opposed to listening for the main idea. To help students achieve success, the instructor may play the lecture more than once. If you want to help students frame the details, focus the first listening on the main ideas and organization of the lecture. Then students will know what section of the lecture will hold the information that they are looking for. The graphs presented in Activity C (discussed in the next paragraph) help students to visualize the same information presented in the lecture. The instructor may find that having students read and understand the graphs prior to the lecture will also help them to succeed in comprehending the lecture.

Activity C presents students with graphs that illustrate the trends in television viewing over the last forty years. By combining the information from the lecture and the graphs, as well as using their background knowledge, students should be able to make statements about lifestyle changes in the lives of Americans. This activity also branches nicely to a discussion regarding how television has changed the society in the students' own countries. Some students may have come from countries where television is still only found in public places, whereas others have come from countries with a technological history much like that of the United States.

Answers

A. 1. L; 2. H; 3. H; 4. H; 5. H; 6. H; 7. L; 8. H; 9. L;
10. H; 11. F; 12. L; 13. H; 14. H

B. 1. 94.2 million; 2. approx. 38%; 3. 4.58 hours; 4. 6.88 hours;
5. 4.42 hours; 6. 3.75 hours; 7. 2.77 hours; 8. approx. 2 hours per day; 9. 1,300 hours per year; 10. 20,000 hours; 11. False;
12. 30%; 13. 50%; 14. 37%

C. Possible answers:
Then: More time to develop outside hobbies/interests; more time for exercise, reading/educating self, conversing with family; less fearful of random violence
Now: Less time to converse with family/friends, to exercise, to develop intellectual interests or hobbies; more fearful of random violence; more informed about world happenings (if viewing includes TV news and analysis); more connected to global issues

Additional/Follow-up Activities

1. Interview a person who grew up without television and one who grew up with television. Compare the lifestyles of the two.
2. Conduct your own poll about television viewing habits. See if the averages reported here are similar to those in your environment. If they are different, discuss what may cause the discrepancies.

III. Television and Education

Techniques

This section explores the controversial attitudes people hold toward the impact of television in their lives. We begin by looking at the impact of television on education. Activities A and B start on a positive note and ask students to describe a time that television positively influenced them. It helps to get students moving in the right direction for the instructor to have a personal example ready to share (or ask a friend to come to share his or her experience). Activity C exposes students to the breadth of educational programming already available (by analyzing only five days of a public television guide). Instructors may want to expand this activity by bringing in an entire monthly guide, dividing up the pages among students and finding out what subjects are covered over the span of a month. Activity D allows students to share the types of educational programming found in their own cultures. This can be informative because many countries conduct language lessons and college courses via the television.

Activities E, F, G, and H all deal with the text "What about *Sesame Street?* How about *Mr. Rogers?*" This text is taken from *The Read-Aloud Handbook* by Jim Trelease, and though Trelease concedes that television can sometimes play a positive role for educators, he also sees it as a danger to the literacy abilities of our children. I find this text valuable in two ways: (1) it suggests some good uses for television in education, and (2) it is a perfect text for teaching students to read critically to infer an author's bias. Activity F is a straight comprehension activity asking students to identify the author's positive statements regarding television's use in education. Activities G and H are designed to help students discover the author's bias through the use of critical reading skills. Because critical reading is an advanced skill, the instructor may want to conduct these activities in class.

Activity I is used to introduce students to one criticism brought against television when talking of its negative impact on education. Again, to have students focus on the meaning of the cartoon, the instructor may want to give groups of students the cartoon separated frame by frame and have them reassemble it in the correct order. Such an activity will require students to deal with the difficult vocabulary found in the first two frames.

Activity J continues to present reasons why some people criticize television's impact on education. Students must read each reason and then choose the supporting details, facts, and examples that best support the reason stated. At this point, the instructor may want to spend some extra time discussing the reasons and the support given. Do students agree with the author's ideas? Which ones seem harder to prove than others? A class discussion of this type will help students to better assimilate the material.

Activity K can be conducted as suggested in the book (with letters to the editor being the final product), or it can be set up as a class debate. If you have students write letters to the editor, it may be helpful to bring in sample letters to the editor to give students some sort of model of expressing their opinions.

Answers

B. Answers will vary.

C. History, geography, political science, economics, taxes, biology/zoology/ecology, literature, classical music, business, the stock market, social issues, biography, civil rights, wartime technology, media studies, European issues

D. Answers will vary.

F. Information that supports the use of television or video as an educational tool
Paragraph 1: "not all television is mindless or violent"; "a two-year study of 326 five- and seven-year-olds that showed viewing of educational television has a positive effect on children's reading"; "On the subject of educational TV, it is my opinion (one shared by many) that *Mr. Rogers,* with its civil, value-oriented focus on children through conversation, is the finest programming for young children today and proves you can hold their attention without car chases or violent robotics."
Paragraph 2: All of paragraph 2 should be underlined.
Paragraph 3: "video can be used effectively to increase 'visual background knowledge.' An inner-city child may not have the visual inventory of the far north that a child in Minnesota does. So if you are reading *Call of the Wild,* by Jack London, a partial showing of the recent *White Fang* video would improve that."
Paragraph 4: "Videos also are an excellent vehicle for teaching the difference between the art forms of film and book. Occasionally, *after* (never before) reading a book, show the video and compare the differences, noting how much was left out and why."
Paragraph 5: Nothing in paragraph 5 should be underlined.

G. Possible answers:

Despite the title, nothing is said about *Sesame Street* in particular. And though a little is said about *Mr. Rogers,* it is only an opinion; no details or facts are presented. I would have liked to see more uses of television for educational purposes, more discussion of how educational TV can help children. The author only tells the conclusion of the PBS study. I'd like to know more of why the study came out so positively.

H. 1.   School board members, parents, teachers/educators
   2.   The answer here is Description A. Hopefully students can see that the audience of the text is not only educators but perhaps primarily parents. As well, though talking of television as an educator, the text has an underlying interest in promoting the skill of reading. Selection B would not be a choice, because the audience and purpose of "What about *Sesame Street?* How about *Mr. Rogers?*" are not as academic in tone as this description. The third selection, C, does describe a text that is written primarily for educators. However, "What about *Sesame Street?* How about *Mr. Rogers?*" includes no program philosophies, learning objectives, or descriptions of appropriate audiences.
   3.   Possible answer:
   The author is giving some positive uses for television at home and in the classroom. But overall, he seems to be somewhat negative on television and very interested in enabling parents and educators to support reading development. In almost every paragraph, reading comes up, though the topic is supposedly television as an educator.
   4.   *Paragraph 1:* "the biggest influence on children's reading development and skills was parent attitudes"
   Paragraph 2: "Your local PBS station can provide you with a complete list of *Reading Rainbow* book titles, one of the best children's book lists available. Once a book . . ."
   I believe that the author's primary interest is to enable parents and teachers with the tools necessary to improve children's reading attitudes and abilities.
   5.   The author has a predominantly negative attitude toward television.
   Paragraph 1: "not all television is mindless or violent"; "though even educational programs hurt when they become substitutes for play or socializing or when viewed to excess—more than ten hours a week"; "proves you can hold their attention without car chases or violent robotics"

Paragraph 3: "Although television and video are easily abused"; "Showing the entire video is usually a waste of valuable class time and an insult to the teacher's salary scale (and to the taxpayer's pocketbook)."

Paragraph 5: "If you wish to prevent mindless viewing . . . and the abuse of VCRs"; "many in the class will slump into a mindless stupor"

I. 1. Calvin is talking about how lightning quick the images on television are. Hobbes concludes that it is because the attention spans of Americans are too short. By the time Hobbes makes his conclusion, Calvin has already started thinking about something else (proving he has a short attention span).
  2. The quickness and unrelatedness of the images making up television commercials
  3. That advertisement producers realize that Americans have an attention span of only one second. Therefore, to keep the audience interested in the commercial, they have to keep changing what's happening on the screen.
  4. If it is true that Americans cannot concentrate on one image for more than a second, educators are at a disadvantage. Skills like reading, lecture listening, and math require concentration for much longer than seconds—they need minutes or hours of concentration.

J. 1. e;   2. c;   3. f;   4. b;   5. d;   6. a;   7. g

K. Answers will vary.

Additional/Follow-up Activities

1. Bring in 5–10 minute clips of various types of educational programming, from children's (e.g., *Barney, Sesame Street*) to adults'. Have students identify the educational objectives being addressed.
2. Ask an educator to come in and express his or her feelings about the impact of television on the children he or she is teaching.
3. Have students develop questions and then interview (these interviews could be taped) children of various ages concerning their attitudes toward television and reading. Students can make conclusions based upon their findings.

IV. Television and Societal Stereotypes

Techniques

This section is meant to expose students to a subtle but very real influence that television has in their lives: the formation and maintenance of stereotypes. Activity A introduces students to the concept by having them examine stereotypes of Americans. The instructor also may want to broaden the discussion to include other nationalities (preferably those represented in the classroom). If the subject is handled with care, students can begin to laugh at the ideas and misconceptions they hold of others. Activities B and C move the conversation to media's role in helping to shape/reflect the societal attitudes. Activity B draws on the students' comprehension skills, whereas Activity C requires students to relate the textual concepts to their own ideas of society.

Activities D, E, F, and G work together to examine the images and portrayals of the elderly in the media. Activity D is used to activate student schema toward the topic and prepare them for the reading. Activity E provides the text and a referencing activity based on the text. Activity F further supports student comprehension of the text by having them work with some of the vocabulary. Once these supportive activities are completed, students will be able to answer the comprehension questions posed in Activity G. I find that Activities E and F are done best as homework and better prepare students for a discussion based on the questions in Activity G.

After students have been introduced to groups mistreated by the media (in this case, women and the elderly), they are ready to conduct their own research on media's treatment of another group of society. I've used this group project to have students collect their own data (through use of questionnaires or surveys about how television has treated the minority group chosen) and to introduce them to library research. If the students aren't acquainted with library research, it is beneficial to spend at least one class period preparing them for what they will encounter in the library. I cover the use of key words in searches (general and specific terms), evaluating a source for appropriateness to a task, etc. Fortunately, this topic has had a lot written about it, and nearly every minority group has had someone research its portrayals in the media. When students also bring in real-life examples from the media (especially television clips), the projects come alive. (However, I don't make this a requirement of the project unless I know the students have access to videotaping equipment.) Because research can be time consuming, you might want to assign the project two to three weeks before you expect the students to make their presentations.

Answers

A. Possible answers:

Americans are rich, overweight, do not respect authority and their elders, are too talkative, too friendly, carry guns, etc. These stereotypes come from encounters with Americans abroad, movie and television portrayals, the reports of friends and neighbors who traveled to America, etc.

B. Women are sex symbols, not intelligent, brainless, only noted for their bodies, not to be taken seriously.

C. Possible answers:

Young girls learn that the way to get attention in society is to flaunt their bodies and that it's not important to develop their minds; women have a hard time getting respect for the work they do that involves their intelligence; men view women as objects; men have a hard time working under a woman; society allows more violence toward women; society loses the full contribution that women could make if they weren't having to do their jobs and fight the negative stereotype at the same time.

D. 1. Answers will vary from culture to culture (and from age group to age group!).
2. Possible answers:
    The elderly walk slowly and carefully; they're frail, tiny, and bent over, have gray hair and thin, mottled skin; they are talkative about topics concerning the past or sick friends.
3. Possible answers:
    Advertisers: Pain relievers and other pharmaceuticals; life and health insurance, etc.
    Programs for the ads: The news, dramas involving the elderly (e.g., *Murder, She Wrote; Matlock*)
4. Answers will vary.
5. Answers will vary.

E. *one:* minority; *them:* the mass media; *It:* the minority overtly made unwelcome by the mass media; *These people:* the elderly, those over age fifty; *their:* radio stations; *them:* media services; *That:* the fact that media services are allotted to suit advertisers; *It:* the fact that media services are allotted to suit advertisers; *it:* stereotyping in the entertainments; *their:* the elderly; *they:* the characters mentioned; *these:* too sweet images of grandparents; *They:* the sweet portrayals of the elderly;

all: absence, parody, idealization, problem drama (problem is minority status); *many:* people; *it:* sexual romance among the elderly; *dramatic difficulties:* not plausibly involved in dramas about suspense, money, power, sex, and death, and people find sexual romance among the elderly distasteful; *less:* less appealing than attracting a younger audience; *they:* older actors

F. 1. overtly; 2. bulk; 3. allotted; 4. dominate; 5. suit;
6. fundamental; 7. loquacious; 8. sugar-coated; 9. mark;
10. parody; 11. retired; 12. plausibly; 13. people of golden age;
14. appealing; 15. established

G. 1. The elderly are everyone over fifty years old.
2. They make up one-third of the newspaper and television audience; they are loyal and consistent; they write the majority of letters to television and radio stations; many have listened to the same station or read the same newspaper all their lives; they read, hear, and see more news reports than younger members of the media audience
3. Media services are allotted to suit advertisers (inferred: since advertisers want to market to a younger crowd, media is designed to attract the young).
4. The entertainments
5. Funny, old, loquacious, senile, sugar-coated
6. Absence (no portrayals of the minority person); parody (the minority is imitated for purpose of ridicule); idealization; problem drama (the problem is being a minority); neutrality
7. The elderly and retired are not believable in roles that have to do with money, power, sex, suspense, and death; the public does not like to see the elderly involved in sexual romance.
8. Elderly characters attract an older audience (which advertisers don't like), and elderly characters have established careers that require a higher pay scale than weekly TV budgets can pay.

H. Projects and findings will vary.

Additional/Follow-up Activities

1. Bring in video clips of minorities presented in television roles. Ask students to identify where in the pattern of minority programming (absence . . . problem drama, neutrality) the minority character appears to fall.

2. Watch the documentary "Color Adjustment." This documentary follows the portrayals of African Americans on television from the beginning of the medium to present. If your local or school media library does not have it, the documentary can be obtained from California Newsreel by calling (415) 621-6196.

V. Television and Violence

Techniques

This section deals with one of the more controversial and complex issues surrounding television: does viewing television violence adversely affect our society? The text selections in this section were chosen to provide students with some of the arguments stated on both sides of the issue.

The cartoon in Activity A begins the section by pointing out one of the more commonly held beliefs about viewing television violence: that it leads to violence in the viewer. The cartoon is meant to get students thinking about the topic. Activity B asks for further student thought because they must choose their own beliefs about each of the statements. I like to have students make their own choices and then play a discussion game I call "Agree/Disagree." I put signs up on two sides of the room; one says "agree" and the other says "disagree." I then read each statement and ask students to stand up and move to the side of the room that reflects their belief about the statement. Students are not allowed to stand in the middle of the room, despite how many "it depends" they may have about the statement. Once students have physically made their stance, I ask different class members to articulate why they are standing on the side they have chosen. Students from the other side are encouraged to question or challenge the points of view spoken. If someone's argument is convincing, a "convinced" student may switch sides at any time but must be able to state why. I find that getting students out of their chairs for this activity sparks much more conversation and participation than I usually get from a class discussion.

Activity C introduces a text written about thirty years ago by a psychiatrist. Though the text is old, the same arguments he states are found in current textbooks that analyze the issue of television and societal violence. Thus, I find the text valuable, but I have students evaluate the source and consider the current situations that won't be addressed in this article due to its age. Activity C leads students through this evaluation. Sometimes I need to guide students in answering question #2. If they aren't able to suspect a bias on the part of a journal named *Television Quarterly,* I bring in other magazines that have a leaning or bias and ask them what stance they would expect. For example: *Nature Conservancy* magazine or *Mother Earth*

News—what most likely is their perspective on the environment versus economic development? What would *Shape* magazine say about fast food? exercise? *Cosmopolitan* about women and workplace equity? After going through some of these scenarios, students can predict that *Television Quarterly* would want to take a positive view toward television's impact on society.

Activities D and E are a bit difficult in that students must not only comprehend the text but then must infer the author's position on the same statements that they discussed in Activity B. Activity F presents the rest of the article but in a scrambled way in which students must identify whether a particular statement is a reason for violence on TV or a positive or negative effect of television violence. Activity G presents the findings of one of the more recent studies conducted regarding television and violence. Activity H has students work with the vocabulary found in the text. Activity I assesses student comprehension of the article. Both Activities H and I can be given as homework in preparation for Activity J. Activity J asks students to use the study findings described in the article to counter the arguments stated. If the instructor wants to provide students with a speaking activity, Activity J can be easily set up as a role play between someone with the opinion stated and someone who has read the most recent research on the topic.

Activity K is based on the real-life tragedy of a small child who played with fire as a result of seeing the behavior of the characters in the cartoon *Beavis and Butthead.* The case study and debate activity are meant to encourage students to select the arguments presented earlier in the section to best counter their opponents. Because there is a wealth of information concerning this topic in the library, the instructor may want to give students time to research other views in support of their side of the debate.

Activity L is provided to give students a chance to reflect upon and synthesize the ideas presented in the chapter.

Answers

A. 1. Most likely, she will be shot by her child.
2. The mother assumes she still has control over the influence that viewing television violence will have on her child, but it's too late, the child has already been influenced!
3. Possible answer: The cartoonist is saying that we may be too late in developing a concern about the impact of television violence on our children.

B. Answers will vary.

C. 1. Possible answer: I hope to find information about the research on the developing mind and viewing television violence. I hope to find out if there is any psychological evidence for believing that viewing violence will lead to committing violence.
2. The article will most likely present a protelevision message.
3. Possible answers:
    The date should concern me. This article is approximately 30 years old, and a lot has changed since the writing of the article. More research has been conducted—perhaps researchers have found something conclusive on the issue. Television programming has changed and become more realistic and violent over the years. Society has changed: more women are working outside of the home, and the time burden on parents results in children left to view television unsupervised. Children are watching more television than ever before. Random violence among teenagers is on the rise. All of this presents a different world than the one of the author.

E. *Agree:* (2), 3, 7, (9), (10)
Disagree: 1, (2)
Not enough information: 4, 5, 6, 8, 9, 10

(The numbers in parentheses indicate that the answer could go either way depending upon the situation presented to the author. #2 would probably depend on whether we were talking about children or adults. Numbers 9 and 10 would depend upon whether the author believes that "honest" violence shows that there are usually consequences to pay for committing a violent act.)

F. 1. 2; 2. 3; 3. 1; 4. 1; 5. 3; 6. 2; 7. 1; 8. 1; 9. 3

H. 1. pervasive; 2. depicted; 3. desensitized; 4. perpetrators;
5. consequences; 6. link; 7. heightens; 8. pose

I. 1. Learning to behave violently, becoming more desensitized to the harmful consequences of violence, and becoming more fearful of being attacked

2. Harm to victims, pain, long-term financial or emotional harm
3. Violence was defined as "threatened or actual portrayals, as well as depictions of the consequences of unseen acts."
4. Premium channels (HBO, Showtime) show the most violence. The broadcast networks showed the least violence.
5. The study included entertainment series, movies, and "reality" programs but excluded sports and the nightly news.
6. *Television industry:* Limit the amount of violence, show more negative consequences, increase number of viewer advisories
   Policymakers: Work on program-blocking technology; any restrictions placed on the industry should take into account the most harmful types of violent depictions
   Parents: Recognize that different types of programs pose different risks, watch TV with your children, critically evaluate television with your children

J. 1. Not so. The majority of television programming, 57 percent, contained some violence. And the manner in which the violence was portrayed could have harmful effects.
2. Maybe not, but academic and behavioral studies have indicated that certain types of violence are more harmful than others. The more you watch violence on television the more you risk learning to behave violently, becoming more desensitized to the harmful consequences of violence, and becoming more fearful of being attacked.
3. Actually, the researchers found that the perpetrators of the violence go unpunished 73 percent of the time.
4. There are many studies of violent acts and their known psychological effects. This study attempted to link the violent acts in the programming with the known psychological effects.
5. Well, if that is true, why don't they show the real-life consequences of that violence? Do you know that 47 percent of violent interactions on TV show no harm to victims, 58 percent show no pain, and only 16 percent show that there are long-term (financial and emotional) consequences to violence?

K. Student responses will vary.

L. Answers will vary.

Additional/Follow-up Activities

1. Further explore the issue of television violence and its impact on society by watching the PBS Frontline documentary, "Does TV Kill?" It can be obtained by writing

    PBS Video
    1320 Braddock Place
    Alexandria, VA 22314
    1-(800) 328-PBS1

Tapescripts

Chapter 1. Communication and Media

II. Media and a Communication Model

Activity B

So far in this course we've discussed different forms of media, as well as their limitations and strengths. This was easy to do because we all have had experience with the different forms of media. Today I'd like to discuss something even more basic . . . the definition of media.

Let me start with a little story. A famous pro football coach was talking to his team during halftime. They were losing the game, and the team wondered what important strategy or new ideas he might have to help them do better in the second half of the game. Instead, he surprised everyone by holding up a football and saying, "This, men, is a football." Of course, pro football players know a football when they see one. Why was he being so obvious? His message was, sometimes we jump to the complex issues before we understand the basics. Just like in this example, in order for us to understand a course on media, we have to understand the basics . . . in this case, we have to decide upon a definition for media and mass medium. In addition, we'll go even more basic and discuss communication in general. What is it? How does it work? How does understanding it help us better understand media?

Many of you may be wondering what *media* is. According to a dictionary, media is the plural form of *medium,* an agency or means of communication. Anything that promotes the communication of a message from one to another is known as a medium. For example, right now I'm using the medium of my mouth and the English language to communicate the definition of a medium.

Many people use the term *media* to refer to a specific type of medium, the "mass media." We can call a medium a "mass medium" if it meets two requirements. First, it must reach many people, and second, it must make use of a technological device to communicate the message.

Let me give you an example of the first requirement: the invention of the printing press by Gutenberg made books a mass medium. Prior to this invention, the information communicated by books could only reach a limited number of people, because there were so few copies available. Thus, the original manuscripts could not be called a mass medium because they could not meet our first requirement: reaching many people. After books began to reach many people, other forms of mass media became available: newspapers, radio, magazines, and television.

Let's now examine our second requirement: mass media requires some sort of technological device, located between the source of the message and the destination. So, although I am using my voice to speak a message to you, my voice cannot qualify as a mass medium because no technology is being used. However, if this lecture were videotaped and broadcast to classrooms all over the country, this would be considered a use of mass media because of the use of technology and the ability for my message to reach many people.

There are many objects in this classroom that qualify as examples of mass media. Perhaps the most obvious is your textbook. An author wrote the content and made use of a word processor and publishing technology (printing presses, photography, etc.), and now you (as well as many other students elsewhere) are able to learn the content from it. Can you think of other examples of mass media in this room?

Let's now turn to the concept of communication. Because media is tied so closely with communication, it is helpful to examine the process of communication. One of the simplest descriptions of the communication process is known as the Shannon-Weaver model. *(Show an OHP transparency of model if possible. If not, draw the model on the blackboard or direct students to the blank model in their book.)*

The three rectangles show what most of us first think of when thinking of the process of communication. We know that there is a source (a person or agency that has something to be communicated), a message in the middle (the information that is communicated), and a destination (the person or agency that receives the message).

What we don't often consider are the steps that take place *between* these three main components of communication: the encoding and the decoding processes. First of all, the source must choose a method of transmitting the message. For instance, the author of your language textbook has *encoded* the message by using the English language and his or her computer. This encoded message is sent to the printer, who uses a technological device, *the book*, to pass the message on to the destination. Before the destination can make any sense of the message, he or she must *decode* the message (understand the language, be able to read, understand the vocabulary and concepts, etc.). If the destination cannot correctly decode the message, the communication process cannot be completed.

Many times the source will find out that his or her message either was not received or was somehow misunderstood through the feedback loop. The destination responds to the message in a way that informs the source that the message was received (or not received as the case may be). Let's use an everyday example . . . Roommate 1 is frustrated because Roommate 2 never helps to clean up the apartment. He or she encodes this message of frustration in the words, "This place is a pit!" hoping that the roommate will get the hint and will volunteer to do some cleaning. Roommate 2 responds, "A pit?! No way, you should see Bob's place, now *that's* a pit!" Through the response (feedback) of Roommate 2, Roommate 1 now knows that the encoded message was not received as intended. The next message will have to be encoded differently if the meaning is to be understood.

You see then, more goes into communication than someone just saying something and someone else hearing it. The way that the message is conveyed and the ability of the destination to effectively interpret the message are critical to successful communication. Let's look at a few more examples.

Okay, let's suppose that an ESL teacher verbally gives an assignment to a beginning group of students at the end of class. The students don't do the assignment because he spoke too fast. What would be a more efficient encoding of the message? [He could write assignment on the board, have students turn to the exercise in the book to be completed and do one as an example before making assignment, among other things . . .]

Here's another scenario. A child at the theater is fidgeting on an adult's lap and says "I'm sweaty." The real message is, "I want down." But because a child doesn't always say what he or she really needs, the adult must interpret.

Look at this one. A government agency sends health-care information to a third world country. All the literature is written in English, a second language of the people. However, the people cannot read or write. Though the language selection was appropriate, the vehicle of the message, written material, was not.

So you can see, the encoding and the decoding processes are important in communication. Now, how does this model relate to media? Media messages must follow the same process between the source and the destination. For instance, the source, such as a journalist, screenwriter, etc., has to encode the message in a way that most effectively communicates. The destination (the newspaper reader, the television viewer) must be able to decode the message for mass media to be of benefit to him or her.

References

Schramm, Wilbur, and Donald Roberts, eds. *The Process and Effects of Mass Media.* Champaign: University of Illinois Press, 1972.

Whetmore, Edward. *Mediamerica.* Belmont: Wadsworth Publishing Company, 1989.

Activity E

(See the text of the Mark Twain story on pp. 12–13 of the student book.)

Chapter 2. Societal Expectations of the Media

Opening Activity

A. It is cloudy and 13 degrees, another cold morning here in mid-Michigan, the windchill is at 0 currently at Lansing's Capital City Airport. The FM 90 forecast for today mostly cloudy with a 50 percent chance of snow, a high near 20, southwest winds around 10 miles per hour becoming northwest 10 to 20. For tonight, mostly cloudy, a 60 percent chance of snow, the overnight low near 5 above, northwest winds 10 to 15. On Wednesday, mostly cloudy with a 40 percent chance of snow, with a high near 20 degrees. The extended outlook, a chance of snow each day for Thursday through Saturday, with highs in the 20s and teens, lows in the teens and single digits.

Copyright 1995 the Associated Press. Reprinted by permission.

B. Folks in Pensacola, Florida, know Tony Piccio as the snake man. He's the guy police or firefighters call when they are confronted by a problem that slithers. Piccio is a roofing company owner by trade, but his heart is in herpetology. When authorities need help, Piccio removes the offending serpent without charge. He releases most of the snakes into the wild, but he says some he keeps in his collection of about 30 reptiles. He says he's only been bitten twice, and each snake snap hospitalized him for about a week. But Piccio says it's people, not snakes, who can be the biggest problem. He recalls getting a call at 3:00 in the morning from a man who said a snake was lurking behind his refrigerator. Piccio reached down and pulled out a handful of . . . electrical cord!

Copyright 1995 the Associated Press. Reprinted by permission.

C. Hi, from Mercer New and Used Cars! Hey, we know that our customers have lives . . . when you shop for a new car, you don't have time to go from lot to lot! That's why Mercer New and Used Cars stocks up on thousands of cars to give you the best selection in town!

And we also guarantee the lowest prices around! Now look at that price on this Grand Am, and how 'bout these '97 Buick Skylarks? You can't beat our prices! Hey, with over a thousand cars and trucks on the lot, and 72 month financing, you'll find what you're looking for at a price to smile about! Mercer New and Used Cars has your next car now!

Chapter 3. What's News?

I. Selecting the News

Activity M

Moderator:	Welcome to *I Disagree*, a show that provides a forum for people with different opinions. Today's topic concerns the media's coverage of Kitty Kelley's unauthorized biography of Nancy Reagan. Some experts consider the release of this book as legitimate media material. Others look at it as a cheap excuse to print gossip.
	Our panelists today speaking against the coverage of Kelley's book are former White House press secretary for Nancy Reagan, Sheila Tate; Manford Bergen, a former editorial page editor at the *Des Moines Register* and currently professor of journalism at the University of Iowa; and David Starr of the *Washington Post*.
	Those in favor of the coverage are Carla Kandel, spokesperson for the *New York Times*; *Newsday* spokesperson Mara Nelson; and the *Los Angeles Times* managing editor, Michael R. McCabe.
	Let's begin by asking Ms. Tate—Why are you against the news coverage given to the release of Kitty Kelley's book?

Ms. Tate:	I think that news agencies have forgotten what news is. News is supposed to be history . . . a history that is written one day at a time. This being the case, future generations should be able to look back at the news written today and get an accurate account of the important issues we are currently facing. But the news outlets of today are so interested in selling papers that they have resorted to printing gossip, not truth. Such media policy will lead future generations to misjudge the history of our times.

In fact, I seriously question the editorial decision of the *New York Times* to legitimize this book with page one coverage. People of the future will think, "Hey, the *New York Times* was a credible, influential paper. If it printed Kelley's allegations, there must be some truth in them." When in reality, Kelley's writing is a peep show disguised as a book. |
Moderator:	Mr. Bergen, do you agree?
Mr. Bergen:	Oh, yes. I also question the *Times* and *USA Today*'s coverage. Look, in the newspaper world, space is king. The more space you give to a story, the more you influence your readers to believe it. Let's look at how these news agencies treated this story in terms of space: the *New York Times* gave it nine inches of its front page and 40 more inches on an inside page. *USA Today,* which typically writes short, two-paragraph stories, gave the Kelley biography story almost the same amount of space as the *Times* did. So much for whether the biography is newsworthy.
Moderator:	Mr. McCabe, how do you respond?
Mr. McCabe:	Let me first respond to Ms. Tate. She asserts that newspapers are supposed to write history a day at a time. I agree with her. What I don't agree with is her definition of history. History is more than just the facts of our time. It is also the events that are shared by the society. And let's face it, when Kelley writes a book it is an "event" kind of thing. The story had all sorts of elements which made it newsworthy: (1) It was a Kitty Kelley book . . . and people are always interested in her work. (2) It was about Nancy Reagan, a public figure that the public wants to know more about. (3) Kelley claimed certain things about the Reagan family itself, as well as relationships that Reagan and his wife had with others. Readers like to know about these things.
Moderator:	Ms. Kandel, do you agree?
Ms. Kandel:	Well, we at the *New York Times* found the story to be newsworthy on two accounts. We believe that the book offered the public some insight as to how Mrs. Reagan influenced the presidency, and we also saw the release of the book as a local story. Don't forget, publishing is a big industry in New York. We thought that this book would be a publishing phenomenon that would catch the entire country's attention. And we were right! Within only three weeks, the book is in its third printing, it has sold one million copies, and it has entered the *New York Times* best-seller list at number one.

Moderator:	Ms. Nelson, why did *Newsday* give the story so much coverage? You ran three lead stories about Kelley's biography the week it was published.
Ms. Nelson:	We felt the prominent coverage was justified. Kelley's biography in and of itself may not be newsworthy. But the controversy that it caused is definitely newsworthy. The public response to the story increased the newsworthiness of the situation. The hoopla surrounding the publication of the book is important, especially given that you're talking about such an important public figure as Nancy Reagan.
Mr. Bergen:	Let me respond to that if I may.
Moderator:	Mr. Bergen.
Mr. Bergen:	The people of *Newsday* and the *Times* keep talking about the "event" caused by this publication; the "hoopla." But they don't seem to recognize that they have created the hoopla by publishing the story in the first place. The question is, was the story newsworthy *prior* to the prominent news coverage it received? I say it wasn't.
Moderator:	Mr. Starr, how do you view this story? We noticed that the *Washington Post* didn't cover the release of Kelley's book.
Mr. Starr:	I think these papers ought to be ashamed of themselves. They stretched the ethical rules of journalism to publish this story.
Moderator:	How so?
Mr. Starr:	When an editor gets a story about someone's private life, he has to look at the source and ask some difficult questions. Who is this source? Does this source have a reputation for credibility? Has the source followed correct procedures in checking to make sure that the information is true and not just hearsay? If these questions cannot be answered satisfactorily, the story should not be printed. The source of the story should be held to the ethical guidelines of your news establishment.
	In this case, the source, Kitty Kelley, is known for her reputation of digging up gossip. She has not shown herself to be a credible investigative journalist. Instead, she accepts information from second- and thirdhand accounts . . . and then doesn't check with those actually involved in the situation to verify the truth of the account. When these newspapers uncritically repeat Kelley's accusations against Mrs. Reagan, they give her work their stamp of approval. And I don't think her work deserves it.
Moderator:	I'm afraid we're out of time. I'd like to thank all our panelists today for their perspectives.

References

Case, Tony. "Is Gossip News?" *Editor and Publisher,* April 27, 1991, 9–11.

Chapter 4. Newspapers

I. The History of American Newspaper Journalism

Activities D and E

Today I'm going to walk you through a history of American newspaper journalism. It is my thesis that American journalism can be divided into five eras. These eras alternate between reporting that is objective and reporting that is subjective, or more opinionated. Let's look at the five eras.

The Early Years

The first era is what I'd like to call the early years. Um, prior to 1700, the early colonists didn't have newspapers; instead, they got their news by means of pamphlets, handwritten letters, a person who would shout the news from the street, known as a town crier, and English newspapers, British newspapers. The first attempt at publishing an American newspaper came in 1690 by Benjamin Harris. But, because Britain controlled the colonists at that time, the governor banned the printing of this American newspaper.

In 1704, the *Boston Newsletter* was printed by John Campbell. This newspaper's main role was to pass on the news that came from the ships that would land at the U.S. coast. Because the majority of the business for the early colonists was tied directly to the shipping industry, this type of news was very important to them. However, tensions continued to grow between the American colonists and England, and the early newspapers reflected this type of political upheaval.

Prior to the Revolution, newspapers were full of opinion pieces discussing whether or not Americans should revolt from British rule or not. However, unlike today's newspapers, which reserve opinion for a special page on the newspaper, the editorial page, these articles of opinion were found on the front pages of the newspapers.

As well, cartoons were also political in nature; they were not for entertainment. A very famous cartoon shows a snake divided into several parts, several sections. Each section was labeled with the name of the colonies of that time. Underneath the snake was a caption that read, "join or die." This of course had the idea that the colonies should join together in a united effort against England um in order to try to fight off the um, the oppression of the British rule that they felt.

Um, the political stance of each newspaper was either pro-England, or prorevolt. This depended upon what was the opinion of the owner-editor. At that time, newspapers were owned by perhaps a highly educated, fairly wealthy individual in the community, and this person would put together his own newspaper and, of course, reflect his own opinions. Um, this type of reporting, which supports one opinion over another opinion, is known as advocacy journalism. The early years were characterized by such a type of advocacy journalism.

Um, after the revolution, the early press continued a political focus. Now instead of the question of whether to revolt or not, or news about the war, the newspapers were filled with other political ideas. Things like, what form should the constitution of the United States take? what do we believe about taxes? um how should the government tax its people? what uh, stance should the United States take in international relations with France and England?

These ideas were usually those of the owner-editors, and they were promoted to the people with their newspapers.

In addition, political parties would sponsor newspapers to ensure that they would speak for their policies. An example is Andrew Jackson, who was one of our presidents. He gave the *Washington Globe* a federal contract making it be the mouthpiece of his ideas.

So you can see that during the early years, um, the early years were characterized by opinion, they were characterized by the opinions of either the owner-editors or of the political parties who would sponsor the newspapers. Again, in the early years, that was the birth of what we call advocacy journalism, supporting one side of an issue over another.

The Penny Press

At the time of the early years, newspapers cost about 6 cents apiece, 6 pennies, and believe it or not, this made newspapers too expensive for the middle class and the lower class. Essentially then, newspapers were the property of the wealthy and the highly educated Americans. Um in 1833, Benjamin Day, who was the publisher of the *New York Sun*, made, he made use of the progress that was being made in industrialization and technology in order to produce a cheaper paper, one that cost only 1 cent. This then, is the birth of what we call the next era of journalism, the penny press.

Because the newspapers were now only 1 cent, newspapers could now reach an audience wider than just the wealthy and the highly educated. As a result, the nature of the news changed. For instance, the common man and woman who could now afford the paper, they weren't so interested in just politics, they were also interested in local news. Especially gossip about local people, fires, crimes committed, marriages, who married who, um, who divorced who, if divorce was to happen, and obituaries, which were notices of death, these were of great interest to the people.

In fact, one of the most popular sections of the *New York Sun* was a section called the "Police Reports." This is a report, uh which would indicate all the stories of people who were arrested, the crimes they committed, how they committed them, how they were arrested, uh, what happened to them as a result of their crime.

Um this is not to say that all subjective news was wiped out of the papers. There were still articles that included opinions about the social issues of the time, and the social issues of this time were slavery, women's rights, and poverty. However, unlike the early papers, opinions were separated from the factual news. One of the first leaders in this technique was Horace Greeley of the *New York Tribune*. He was the first to create what we now know as the editorial page, the section reserved for opinion about current issues. So he would put the opinion on the editorial page, but the front page would be filled with factual news. As a result, people began to look at the newspapers during the time of the penny press as being much more objective than that of the early press. Newspapers also began to separate other news into sections as well. During the penny press era, sections we now expect in our current newspapers were first created. Sections such as the finance section, religion section, society, arts, these kinds of things were put in separate sections of the newspaper during the penny press.

Um, the public also wanted access to current international and national news. Okay, remember this is a time, actually, before television or radio, and though telegraph existed, it was a new and expensive technology. Most news was brought by hand, over the sea, by shipping vessels. So, how could an editor be sure to get all of the news for his readers? As well, the editor was thinking, if he could get the news first, more people would buy his newspaper. So the answer that most editors used in order to get the news first was to place messengers all along the U.S. coast. It was these messengers' job to gather the news from the sea captains and travel back to the editor with it. We call these types of messengers "couriers," okay? However, such a plan was expensive, you can imagine if you had to have people in every major city um, stationed to try to get news from every boat that came in and had to rush back up to New York City with the news, that this would take some amount of expense.

The New York newspapers realized that they were spending a lot of money trying to be the first to publish international news. As a result, six of the New York newspapers joined together to share the cost of telegraph services to transmit the news. This agreement meant that they would be all guaranteed to receive national and international news at the same time. This telegraph service is what we now call the Associated Press, or the AP. In fact, if you look at your newspaper now, a current newspaper, you'll find that many articles will have the initials "AP" at the top of the article. This indicates that uh this particular article came from what we call the wire services, or the news service, the Associated Press.

This Associated Press idea caught on with other newspapers all over the country, not just New York. Soon the AP was supplying articles in both the South and the North of the U.S. As membership grew, the more objective the news had to become in order to maintain the subscription of all the customers. For instance, at this time the Civil War was beginning to heat up, um, the AP had to be careful that their stories were not too proslavery or too antislavery, because if it was one way or another, they would lose the audience of either the South or the North. And because they were interested in the money they were making, they didn't want to lose any of their audience; therefore, they made sure that their stories tried to uh, approach the issues of the . . . that were um, uh facilitating the Civil War, they tried to approach these things with more of an objective stance.

Okay, let me recap now, the penny press. Because of having a wider audience, since more people could buy a 1 cent newspaper, the articles became less political. Also during that time, the opinion pieces were separated from factual news and put into a separate page called the editorial page. As well, um during that time, uh the Associated Press was born, and because of the Associated Press's desire to make money and keep as many subscribers to their service as possible, they also ran a more objective type news service. Um, so you see that because of all these different factors, the penny press was more objective than the early years of newspapers.

Yellow Journalism

Okay, now I'd like to head into a time of journalism probably known as the lowest period of American journalism. This period is known as yellow journalism. After the Civil War, this type of journalism, or sensational journalism, was born. The name "yellow journalism" came because of the fierce competition between two newspaper owners, Joseph Pulitzer and William Randolph Hearst. Both owned New York newspapers, and both fought to get the best circulation from the New York market. Their competition was so fierce that Hearst hired the best reporters and cartoonists away from Pulitzer's paper. At that time, Pulitzer had a cartoonist named Richard Outcault, who produced the "Yellow Kid" cartoon, which depicted humorous

New York scenes and situations. This was a very famous cartoon; many people in New York loved the cartoon, and some would even buy that newspaper to be able to read what the Yellow Kid was doing next. Hearst hired him away from Pulitzer. Pulitzer responded by just hiring a different artist to do the same "Yellow Kid" cartoon. This meant that New York now had two newspapers with two "Yellow Kid" cartoons. This is where we got the name of yellow journalism.

Um, however, this type of journalism is more than just competition between two newspaper owners. What made it be considered, um, the lowest time of American journalism is that the journalism was characterized by sensational stories, what we call "flashy" headlines, headlines that make you want to read the story but maybe don't reflect the truth of the story. Pictures were brought into papers at this time. Color printing was brought in, and the stories seemed to focus much about sex, scandals and crime. They also focused on what we would call publicity stunts. These stunts began with ethical ideas. For instance, Pulitzer had his reporters take the role of investigators who were to expose corruption found in society. A famous example is when one reporter pretended to be insane. By pretending to be insane, she was admitted into the state mental institution, or what we call the state asylum. As a result, she was able to gain firsthand knowledge of the horrid conditions inside of that institution. Her, uh, the articles that she was able to write as a result of having this experience, um, helped to change how the mentally ill were treated. This, we could say, is a good use of journalism. However, the act of faking insanity is considered a little bit unethical.

However, as the circulation wars heated up, the papers began to use information in a very unethical way. One example is the story of the conditions in Cuba prior to the Spanish-American War. Pictures were printed in the papers to portray the misery of Cubans uh, that they faced under the Spanish control. Some of these pictures were true, but others were just fakes.

In addition, after about a year of obvious support for a war with Spain, Hearst blew up a story about a woman named Evangelina Cisneros, who was the niece of the Cuban revolutionary president, who'd been jailed for her antigovernment activity. He devoted a lot of space in his newspaper to her story, 375 columns, and as a result was able to gain a lot of U.S. support for her well-being. He then sent a reporter in order to rescue her, and he then reported the details of the rescue. Later it was revealed that she had agreed to voluntary minimum security house arrest, and the treatment that she had received in jail had been exaggerated by the papers in order to make a better story. This is an example of how Hearst would take an insignificant news item and would manipulate the truths surrounding it in order to gain a larger reading audience. In fact, many people now believe that the Spanish-American War was, in some ways, engineered by Hearst and Pulitzer in order to increase the circulation of their newspapers.

The Objective Years

Well you can imagine that this kind of feeling among the people, that solely for capital gain, um, people would engineer news in order to gain support for a war, that most people started to um, resent this type of reporting. It's true that yellow journalism sold papers. But people began to get tired of it. Libraries and community leaders, in reaction to the focus on sex and crimes, canceled their subscriptions to yellow newspapers. In addition, at that time, there was the assassination of President McKinley. Many people believe that Hearst's blatant attacks of the president in his newspaper were partly to blame for the killing. It was said that an anti-McKinley article from Hearst's paper was found in the pocket of the man who killed him. So these kinds of things led people away from yellow journalism, and as a result, journalism began to take a turn toward objectivity.

Um, it's at this time, that what . . . the era I called objective journalism came to be. Um, some newspapers had all along held to objective standards throughout the yellow journalism era. One such man was Adolf Ochs, the owner of the *New York Times.* When he purchased the newspaper, it was in danger of going under; it almost didn't survive. He, however, he was able to save the newspaper without resorting to yellow journalistic techniques. In fact, he would print speeches, treaties, and government documents in their entirety, which became the true symbol of objectivity.

At the same time, journalism was growing as a profession. Journalism schools were being established, and these schools were promoting the idea of proper reporting involving the attempt of objectivity. In 1923, the American Society of Newspaper Editors upheld the standard that "a journalist who uses his power for any selfish or otherwise unworthy purpose is faithless to a high trust."

Because of such standards, journalism began to become more and more objective. This led to a change in reporting. Journalists became careful. They started reporting both sides of an issue, and they seemed to check their facts and their figures with multiple sources before printing their stories.

Another development in the media industry contributed to this emphasis on objectivity. Before, ownership of newspapers was individual, it was local owners, um, men like Hearst or Pulitzer, who were the owners of the newspapers. However, now the ownership of the newspapers was changing to corporations, places like Gannet and um Newhouse, corporations named Gannet and Newhouse. These corporations bought the major newspapers of U.S. cities. Because their interest was profit, money, not necessarily politics, the reporters weren't then pressured to slant their stories.

So let me recap the years of objective journalism. Objective journalism came as a result of the distaste people had toward yellow journalism and the types of stories that people were exposed to then. Uh, people at that time began to try to show that they were more objective than others. For instance, Adolf Ochs tried to print documents in their full pieces, in their entirety, in order to show that he wasn't cutting out important information. As well, there were schools that were promoting objectivity in the journalism schools, and the ownership of newspapers changing to corporations also promoted objectivity.

New Journalism

Okay, let's now move to the last era of newspaper journalism in the United States. This last era is what we would call new journalism. This type of journalism was born out of the frustration um that objective reporting assumes that there are only two sides to an issue. It ignores the fact that most issues are more complex than just having two sides. Journalists began to struggle with the concept of objectivity in reporting due to the McCarthy hearings in the 1950s. Joseph McCarthy was a Wisconsin senator who accused many citizens of being communists. It became clear to journalists that facts weren't enough to present a story. The experienced reporters felt that they could make value judgments about the facts as well as just report them.

Um, in 1958 the AP and now a new news service called the UPI began to put out more interpretive stories. Um, and by the 1960s there were a few journalists who experimented with a more subjective reporting. What they did is they allowed their emotions and point of view to become part of the story. The goal of these reporters was to try to present a picture of the event from inside the mind of the source, rather than just tell about the event by giving facts. Such writing was generally published in books, magazines, and underground newspapers. But occasionally it could be found in more standard newspapers. It has left its influence on many of the papers of today in the form of soft news. Now many major newspapers print objective stories with a soft news analysis of the story side by side.

Well, these are the five eras, and they seem to be going from objective, to subjective, back to objective again, and now we're in a more subjective type of newspaper journalism. Um, please look at the evidence and see if you think so yourself. Thank you.

References

Emery, Edwin. *The Press and America: An Interpretive History of the Mass Media.* Englewood Cliffs: Prentice-Hall, 1984.

Mott, Frank. *American Journalism, A History.* New York: Macmillan Publishing Company, 1962.

Whetmore, Edward. *Mediamerica.* Belmont: Wadsworth Publishing Company, 1989.

Chapter 5. Radio

I. The Golden Age of Radio

Activity F

Chicago Morning

It was a cold winter morning in Chicago. Paul was sound asleep in his warm bed. Outside the strong northeast wind blew across the lake, and the window shutters beat rhythmically against the house. Suddenly, the radio alarm went off. From a distant room, the phone rang. Sleepy Paul sat up quickly in bed, yawned, and stretched. Then he jumped up, and hit the radio alarm clock. He looked out the windows and heard a train and, in the distance, the sound of a fire engine bell. Again the phone rang, and he stumbled across the room, bumping his leg on the bed as he went and scaring his dog. He picked up the phone and said "Hello." But no one answered. All he heard was a low and dull dial tone. Paul slammed down the phone and prepared himself for another day in the city.

II. Modern Radio Formats

Activity L

News

A. Good morning it's 22 minutes after 8:00, I'm Shannon Morris at your 106 second up-date. . . . Pardon me. The newspaper unions on strike against Detroit's two newspapers have rejected the latest return to work offer. The unions voted no to the company's four-point offer which includes paying for job training for workers replaced by new hires during the strike. The unions say they'll go to the national labor relations board to force the newspapers to hire back all the striking workers.

The weather forecast from Andy is coming up next, I'm Shannon Morris with your 106 second update from Q106.

From Q106 FM. Reprinted by permission.

B. Here's what we're following for you this noon in the newsroom. Jury deliberation could start this afternoon in the talk show slaying case. Shiawassee County police are still trying to determine if human remains found yesterday near Bancroft belong to a man murdered on Super Bowl Sunday. Secretary of State Warren Christopher is due at any moment to announce his resignation. And what do Americans expect from the president out of his second term? We'll have responses from the people, and more, after Paul Harvey on WITL.

From WITL FM. Reprinted by permission.

C. President Clinton has reportedly chosen North Carolina businessman Erskin Bolds for the job of chief of staff. He will succeed Leon Panetta, who is returning to his home state of California, possibly to run for governor.

Indian air force planes and helicopters are staging an emergency airlift of food and medi-cine to half a million stranded people. The southeast Indian coast is reeling from a cyclone Wednesday night that killed at least a thousand people. The death toll is expected to climb. Winds were clocked at up to 100 miles per hour.

From WKAR FM. Reprinted by permission.

Advertising

A. You're tuned to WKAR FM. Michigan State University's Department of Theater is proud to present Tony Kushner's acclaimed *Angels in American*—Part 1, *Millenium Approaches,* this Thursday, that's tomorrow on the Festival Stage of the Wharton Center. It begins at 8:00. *Angels* is considered by many in the literary and dramatic communities to be the best play written in the last 50 years. You'll have an opportunity to see it here on the MSU campus. And by the way, this play contains adult themes, language, and more. It is not suitable for children or teenagers. If you'd like more information, call 355-6690, that's 355 sixty-six, ninety.

From WKAR FM. Reprinted by permission.

B. More concert information from Lansing's concert station. The storm rises again as rock's true colors emerge . . . Deep Purple, in concert. America concert series presents, December 5 at the Palace of Auburn Hills . . . on stage for the first time in over a decade the power reignites! One of the influential bands of all time returns . . . Deep Purple. Tickets go on sale this Saturday morning at 10:00. At the Palace box office, all Ticketmasters including Harmony House and Blockbusters Music. Now the return . . .

From Q106 FM. Reprinted by permission.

C. Well it's true, there's always something exciting happening in terms of bargains, real bargains, at Midwest Furniture Clearance Centers, but you will see announced in your paper tomorrow that this will be the final weekend that you can take advantage of those incredible special credit terms during Midwest Furniture Clearance Center's Half Off and More Sale tomorrow. 10 to 9 for the final weekend. Just load up! Everything's at least 50 percent off, some items up to 75 percent off at Midwest Furniture Clearance Centers, plus you don't pay for over a year. You just don't pay till 1998! Tomorrow, 10 till 9, Midwest Furniture Clearance Centers, no down payment, no interest, no payments till January 1998 to qualified buyers. Ask for details at the sale.

From WITL FM. Reprinted by permission.

Deejay Banter

A. Q106, music for the X Generation, the Y Chromosomes, the Ink Tunes, the G Spies, the CIA, the FBI . . . WJXQ, Jackson, Lansing, smack dab in the middle of another Q106 in a row!

From Q106 FM. Reprinted by permission.

B. Folks in Pensacola, Florida, know Tony Piccio as the snake man. He's the guy police or firefighters call when they are confronted by a problem that slithers. Piccio is a roofing company owner by trade, but his heart is in herpetology. When authorities need help, Piccio removes the offending serpent without charge. He releases most of the snakes into the wild, but he says some he keeps in his collection of about 30 reptiles. He says he's only been bitten twice, and each snake snap hospitalized him for about a week. But Piccio says it's people, not snakes, who can be the biggest problem. He recalls getting a call at 3:00 in the morning from a man who said a snake was lurking behind his refrigerator. Piccio reached down and pulled out a handful of . . . electrical cord!

Copyright 1995 the Associated Press. Reprinted by permission.

C. It's 9:54! Hey, that's right where you hear the new music first on this radio station— That is a wild one isn't it? It's by request for uh, Tom Proft? no, no relation to the guy that used to work here in the news department . . . but down in Jackson today, he loves hearing that song and wants to do that on his way to work! If you're listening while you work, we appreciate that too . . . that's called "Cherokee Boogie"! And that just about wraps it up here . . .

From WITL FM. Reprinted by permission.

Weather

A. Mid-Michigan weather! Exclusive News 10 forecast for all of mid-Michigan, including Haslett and Holt! Today, periods of rain, heavy at times, high 55 and falling after that. Scattered showers for tonight, some clearing possible late tonight. Temperatures down to 32 for the low and then a mixture of clouds and sun tomorrow. Could be some showers too, with a high of 47. Light rain, 45 right now at the Lansing Capital City Airport.

From WITL FM. Reprinted by permission.

B. Q106 weather from Andy, becoming cloudy and windy today, looking for a high of 45. Rainy and windy tonight, low dropping down to 40, right now it is 20 in Lansing, and Andy is telling us it's going to be a crappy, crappy weekend . . . winter's coming back, we'll get the details in just a little while.

From Q106 FM. Reprinted by permission.

C. It is cloudy and 13 degrees, another cold morning here in mid-MI, the windchill is at 0 currently at Lansing's Capital City Airport. The FM 90 forecast for today mostly cloudy with a 50 percent chance of snow, a high near 20, southwest winds around 10 miles per hour becoming northwest 10 to 20. For tonight, mostly cloudy, a 60 percent chance of snow, the overnight low near 5 above, northwest winds 10 to 15. On Wednesday, mostly cloudy with a 40 percent chance of snow, with a high near 20 degrees. The extended outlook, a chance of snow each day for Thursday through Saturday, with highs in the 20s and teens, lows in the teens and single digits.

Copyright 1995 the Associated Press. Reprinted by permission.

III. An Influential Format: Talk Radio

Activity N

Interview One

Interviewer: Hi, we're interviewing people for a radio industry survey today, and the purpose is to assess the impact of the *Rush Limbaugh Show* on the general public. Would you mind answering a few questions for me?

Person 1: Sure.

Interviewer: First, could you give me your overall opinion of Rush Limbaugh?

Person 1: Oh, I can't stand him, I hate watching his show. I have a brother-in-law who used to watch the show all the time and so . . . or listen to the show all the time and so I'd listen too, and I'd listen for about 15 minutes before I'd just have to leave the room.

Interviewer: How did you come to this opinion?

Person 1:   Well, basically from this experience of listening to it when my brother-in-law was listening to it, and I would just listen to the things he would say and compare them to what I know about politics and what's going on in the world and just— there was no matchup . . . I just really disliked hearing what he had to say.

Interviewer: Are there any of his, uh, ideas that you do agree with?

Person 1:   Well, yeah, I mean oftentimes he'll say things that make sense along the way, but um, so there are little details and things that I'd agree with, but his overall perception of how he puts these bits and pieces together just does not match my view of the world at all.

Interviewer: Ok, um can you give me an idea of some of his ideas that you disagree with?

Person 1:   Well, his whole perception of of, economics, for example, he really is one who believes in the American dream, that if you work hard enough you'll achieve whatever you want, and anyone who doesn't achieve what they want it's simply because they're not working hard enough . . . But he just doesn't have any perspective on the fact that he is a really privileged white man in this society, and that, yes, for him the American dream can come true. But there are a lot of people who are discriminated against because of the color of their skin or their sexual orientation or because they grew up in poverty in the first place, who just can't reach that dream, and he doesn't seem to have any compassion or understanding or perspective about that at all.

Interviewer: Do think that he's had an impact on American politics?

Person 1:   Unfortunately, I would say yes, because he's a very dynamic person, and when he gets on the radio, people like to tune in, I think, just because he has a lot of energy and vitality and he draws a picture of the world that I think people want to believe in, because it's a simple black and white view that people can grab onto really easily, and so people listen to him, and they listen to the narrow way that he presents information, and they think that it all makes sense. They think that, yes, this is the way that the world works, it's nice and easy and simple and I can just make these vast generalizations and I can uh, look at one little detail in isolation from others and make it look like I'm justified in the way I live my life too. So, I think he's very persuasive in that way, and people um, I think have tuned into his show a lot, and he's made the whole genre of radio talk shows really popular. And so a lot of people listen to him, and most, unfortunately, a lot of the radio talk show hosts out there are equally as conservative and narrow minded as he is, and so it's just gotten to a point where people can flip on the radio and listen to language of intolerance and narrow-mindedness that makes them look good. And I'm talking, them, I'm talking about generally conservative, white people in this country, and they love it! And I think it motivates them to go to the polls and vote and it motivates them to call their politicians and express their point of view.

Interviewer: This is pretty closely related to my last question, but do you think that uh he's impacted or influenced society in general, or how do you think he's impacted society in general rather than just specifically politically?

Person 1:   Um, well, I think that outside of the political realm he probably hasn't had that much impact. Um, as I said, I think that his biggest impact on society is making the radio call-in show a really popular forum for people, and that's probably changed society somewhat, that people can just tune in on the radio and listen to opinions being expressed and call up and agree or disagree with the opinions. Um, but in, outside of politics, I really don't see that he's had that much influence.

Interviewer: Okay, well that's all the questions that I have, do you have any other comments?

Person 1:   Oh, just that I wish people would listen to him less . . . simply because I think that he is so narrow minded and that people don't get a broad perspective, they don't get the whole picture when they listen to Rush Limbaugh, so I wish people would listen to people who are more open minded, more intelligent, and have a broader perspective on politics in America.

Interviewer: Okay, thank you.

Person 1:   Thank you.

Interview Two

Interviewer: We're interviewing people for a radio industry survey today. The purpose of this survey is to assess the impact of the *Rush Limbaugh Show*. Would you mind answering a few questions for me?

Person 2:   Uh, no.

Interviewer: First, could you give me your overall opinion of Rush Limbaugh?

Person 2:   I think that Rush is a very, he's a very outspoken man who is sometimes taken . . . a lot of people have interpretations of him when they don't really listen to him, and he's taken out of context a lot, but I think all in all he's uh, a basic guy and he just is very outspoken, and a lot of his beliefs a lot of people don't like.

Interviewer: Can you give me an example of any of his ideas that you agree with, personally.

Person 2:   Uh, I think I agree with his ideas that the uh, the government has gotten too large, and that people should be taking more responsibility for their own actions and looking out for their fellow people in the community, rather than always waiting for the government to come in and to handle the situations. Uh, I think also— well I think his ideas again on the government of just— so reducing the size of the federal government— uh, his idea of getting the balanced budget, we can't just keep spending more and more money, I mean, otherwise, you know, where does it end? I mean where do we finally stop spending the money? And it's going to be some hard choices, but I think we have to face reality that we're going to have to make some hard choices and we don't have unlimited pockets. So I think, again, I think that his ideas of limiting the regulations of government, not necessarily doing away with all of them, but at least limiting them, letting people be in charge of their lives uh and being responsible and trying to balance the budget and making some hard choices, cutting spending in those areas where we can, I agree with those ideas.

Interviewer: Uh, can you give me an example of some ideas of his that you would disagree with?

Person 2: Uh, I disagree with his ideas on the environment. Uh, I think in some cases, uh, he may not totally understand the issues of what's happening with the environment and the ecology and so, I definitely disagree with him there. Uh, in terms of clear-cutting and stuff like that I uh, disagree with him and endangered species.

Interviewer: Can you think of any ways that he has impacted American politics, or do you think that he has impacted American politics?

Person 2: I think he has impacted American politics, for one thing, I think he has made people, he's made a certain group of people who may have felt like they were— nobody was speaking up for them, that they have become emboldened by him, 'cause they feel like he's their representative, uh they feel that the media at large does not represent their viewpoint, and they feel that Rush Limbaugh represents that, so they have embolden— he has emboldened them to speak up, to express themselves more openly, and so I think in that sense, he has impacted it. And he's made people also uh, question everything they he—, question stuff more often that they hear coming from the government, so yeah, I think he has impacted it.

Interviewer: Do you think that he's had any impact on society as a whole?

Person 2: Um, in this, getting it away from politics, how do you separate those two? I think, yeah, one way he's definitely had an impact on society is there's now become this, you know and a lot of people talk about the so-called dittoheads and the groups that follow Rush, but there's also I think just as important, a big group of people who are very anti–Rush Limbaugh, and you know, they get their kicks out of bashing him, uh so I think he has impacted it in that way, whether that's for a positive or a negative, I'm not for sure. Uh, again, I think it's just made people become more aware of— of the news that they hear, uh, questioning you know, what have they been told, what have they not been told, uh so in that sense, I guess as far as society goes too, he's— I think he's impacted it.

Interviewer: Aside from what we've already talked about, do you have any general comments of your own about Rush Limbaugh?

Person 2: Um, I guess the thing— my own feeling about Rush Limbaugh is, you have to take him with a grain of salt. I think he is an alternative news source, uh, but just like anything, you shouldn't listen to only one source of information, you should hear a variety of sources because, you have to face it, people have only so much time to report the news, and face it, they bias the news, whether they're intending to or not by what they do report or how they report something. Or what they don't report. And so I think he is an alternative source where you may hear stuff that you won't hear in other sources, so I— I appreciate that about him. On the other hand, I sort of get tired of— of some of the jokes and I recognize that he may be doing this to sort of goad people, but I do get tired of his flamboyancy, uh, it gets a little bit old, so— So, even though I listen to him occasionally, I usually find that after about 30 minutes or so, I usually have to turn it off.

Interviewer: Okay, thanks a lot for your comments.

Person 2: Thank you.

Interview Three

Interviewer: We're doing a survey for the radio industry to assess the impact of the *Rush Limbaugh Show*. Would you mind answering a few questions for me?

Person 3: Yeah, sure.

Interviewer: First, could you give me your overall opinion of Rush Limbaugh?

Person 3: Well, I couldn't call myself a big fan of Rush Limbaugh, um, although I have listened to him to some degree. Uh, I think he's very good at what he does, but I also think he preaches to the converted for the most part, and um, he plays very fast and loose with the truth.

Interviewer: Okay, which of his ideas do you agree with, would you say?

Person 3: Um, well, I think there's a germ of truth in a lot of what he says, I think some of the things he talks about that the Congress does in the ways that they spend money sometimes is a little more than what they need to do, and the extremes that some liberals go to in order to promote their causes, but on the other hand, there's just as many or more conservatives that go to even more extremes in order to push their causes, so I think even when I agree with um, the— the crux of what he says, I think he only talks about that in terms of one group of people, not um what's done by both conservatives and liberals in the government.

Interviewer: Which of his ideas would you say that you disagree with?

Person 3:   Um, well, I very much disagree with his view of American society in terms of the economy and um, his view that um, if you can make it in America, great, if you can't, tough luck. I think that he has a lot of supporters in big business and he has a lot of supporters in the more conservative branches of government, and he tends to play to Wall Street and to play to big business and those people strengths, and I think he doesn't really have much concern for regular Americans who may have other concerns and other situations in their life.

Interviewer: Can you give me any examples of how you think he may have impacted American politics?

Person 3:   Uh, I think he's impacted American politics a lot, I think he had a big influence on the 1994 election that brought the conservatives uh, into the majority in Congress, at that time he was very popular and his rhetoric at that time was rhetoric that seemed to be more prominent across the country in all forms of the media. And so in that regard I think he has a lot to do with the makeup of the Congress that we see today.

Interviewer: Okay, this is similar but different. How do you think he may have impacted society in general?

Person 3:   Well, I think he's contributed a lot to um the lack of civility in public discourse, which is um sort of a problem in our country. I think he's uh, a very abrasive sort of person, especially with people who don't agree with his ideas, uh and I think that's being seen as more and more acceptable, not only in the media but also in everyday life, and uh, the discourse that we see everywhere, so I think his brand of um journalism and his brand, his style of presenting his point of view impacts the society of the country.

Interviewer: Okay, aside from the questions that I've asked you, do you have any general comments on Rush Limbaugh?

Person 3:   Um, well uh, I hear his popularity has been going down recently, and that could be possibly a sign of the times that um people are moving away from the very, very conservative ideas that are being presented in Congress, and um maybe everybody on both sides is moving towards the middle. So, maybe Rush Limbaugh who is somebody I don't consider to be anywhere near the middle is uh on his way out!

Interviewer: Okay, thank you very much.

Person 3:   Thank you.

Interview Four

Interviewer: Hi, we're interviewing people today for a radio industry survey. The purpose of the survey is to assess the impact of the *Rush Limbaugh Show*. Would you mind answering a few questions for me?

Person 4:   Sure!

Interviewer:	First off, what's your overall opinion of Rush Limbaugh?
Person 4:	Well, you know, a lot of my friends dislike him, but I actually don't think he's that bad! I think he's entertaining. He's got these crazy songs that— granted, they are kind of "in your face," but they are funny to listen to— they're no different to me than *Saturday Night Live*'s type of humor.
Interviewer:	Okay. How— how do you come to this opinion, would you say?
Person 4:	Um, well, I have to say I don't listen to him all that much, but at, sometimes when I'm driving, um to and from picking my son up at day care, that's when he happens to be on, and so I hear maybe little bits and snippets of him, I don't hear a whole program, I've never heard a whole program of his, but um, just from that, I would say that.
Interviewer:	Okay, can you tell me about any ideas of his that you would say you agree with.
Person 4:	Well, um, I would have to say that I feel that uh, network media is a bit on the um liberal side, and um, so I do agree with him, he definitely feels that media is liberal, and he probably more— believes it more than I do, but um, but I do think he has a leaning there that is correct. I think the media does um— they seem to leave liberals alone as far as being really tough on them, but for conservatives, they really question them deeply, make them really um um have to answer tough, tough questions that I don't hear them asking the same kinds of questions of liberals.
Interviewer:	Can you tell me about any of his ideas that you disagree with?
Person 4:	Um, I definitely dislike his stance on the environment. I— I feel he overstates— uh, there's parts of what he says is true— I do think we have to find a balance between business interests and um, economic interests and the environment. There has to be some sort of balance there, but he overstates it to the point that I think people will just keep clear-cutting forests, and they don't seem to recognize that there is, I think, a looming crisis in the environment, and I don't think Rush, um helps that cause at all.
Interviewer:	Can you think of any ways that Rush may have impacted American politics?
Person 4:	Well, I feel that the— he definitely is Republican, um, I don't know if he's ever stated that, but he— he must be, by the things he says and the people he supports. Um, and I'm suspicious that the '94 elections were influenced by some of what he said. But I'm also suspicious that the people who listen to him would have voted that way anyway. Um, so I don't know, I guess my answer's kind of ambiguous, I feel that he does have a conservative leaning and gives good arguments for conservatives to talk to their friends, they can maybe come up with some good arguments that they've heard on his show, but um, I think they would have probably voted the same way whether they listened to him or not.
Interviewer:	Okay, similarly, do you think he's had an impact on the American society in general?

Person 4:   Um, probably, well, maybe in some kind of pop-culturish way. For instance, I think right now the popularity of talk radio. This is, I don't know if it's just going to be a flash-in-the-pan–type thing, but um, right now, talk radio seems to be very popular, and a lot of AM stations are going to that format, and um, I think people like Rush sort of helped that along. However, that might end. You know, I think uh, radio formats come and go, and who knows how long this kind of a thing would last?

Interviewer: Okay. Do you have any general comments of your own, aside from what we've talked about, that you'd like to make about Rush Limbaugh?

Person 4:   Um, you know, a lot of people say they really dislike his abrasive nature, and they feel like he has perhaps put that kind of attitude into the public discourse. And I actually think that kind of nature has been there for a while. Like I mentioned earlier, I think his humor is a lot like *Saturday Night Live,* and um, I think people in America like that abrasive humor. They like um, somebody really sort of diggin' into the other side. And uh, they laugh at it, and uh, we've been laughing at that for a long time on our talk shows, evening talk shows, and evening comedy, and I think uh, Rush is just sort of following along with that.

Interviewer: Okay, thank you very much.

Person 4:   Okay.

Chapter 6. Television

I. Television Programming

Activity F

Carol: Hey Pat! Whatcha doing tonight? Wanna come over and watch TV?

Pat: Sure, but what are you gonna watch? Tonight's my favorite, *ER.*

Carol: You're kidding, aren't you? You like that show more than *Seinfeld?* I don't believe it!

Pat: Yeah, why are you so shocked? It's a great show. It's so realistic . . .

Carol: That's exactly why I don't like it! Who needs all that true-to-life suspense? It's like you have to brace yourself all the time . . . you know that something bad is going to happen somewhere in each show . . .

Pat: It's not as bad as you make out . . . the show is just trying to reflect more of reality. Do you know that all of the episodes are based on things that have really happened in the emergency room of hospitals? I like it because it's engaging, the issues they deal with are current. Also, you really start to know and care about the characters. Most of all, once it's over, it makes me think.

Bryan: Hi, Pat. Hi, Carol. Whatya doing?

Pat: Hi, Bryan. We're trying to decide what to watch tonight. (to both) I don't care what else we watch, but I don't want to miss *ER*.

Carol: Bryan, can you believe that Pat likes *ER* better than *Seinfeld?* She actually likes that reality drama stuff!

Bryan: Well . . . I hate to side with her, Carol, but it sure is better than the shows you watch . . . their plots are improbable . . . the writers always put the characters in such ridiculous situations! They seem pretty lame to me.

Carol: But that's the point! They're not supposed to make you think deeply or anything like that . . . they're just supposed to make you laugh. I don't know about you two, but when I watch TV, I want to be entertained . . . period. I don't want to know about how the health care system is so flawed or how police departments are corrupt or under-staffed . . . I just want to relax when I watch TV.

Pat: What shows do you like, Bryan?

Bryan: I don't really like much that's on TV . . . it's all either brainless or violent . . . but I do find shows like *Wild Kingdom* and *Discovery* educational.

Pat: Yeah, but they're also violent!

Bryan: What do you mean?

Pat: Those nature shows always have one animal killing another. I saw one where an alligator grabbed a poor little deer from the edge of the swamp . . . it was so sad.

Carol: Yeah, it's like the kill is the climax of the show! True, they give you some information about the particular animal species, but then, they always have to show the animal either eating another or being eaten. It's gross!

Bryan: I hate to tell you this, but that's life in the wilderness. Survival of the fittest . . . It's *true* reality programming! Besides, when you're done with the show, you leave more informed than before. I like that I can learn from my time in front of the TV.

            Hey, what are we doing talking? It's time for *Star Trek, Next Generation!*

Pat: Great! I love that show!

Carol: Me too!

II. The Predominance of Television

Activity B

Good afternoon. This week we've been discussing the impact of media in our society . . . Today we're going to look at one of the more influential media—television.

Most of you have grown up with television; you don't remember a time without television in your lives. But perhaps you're not aware of the scope of the influence television has held in the average American's life.

Consider this. In 1950 only 4.6 million homes in America had one television. By 1960, that number had jumped to more than tenfold; 45.2 million homes had one television set, and of those, 5.4 million homes had more than one set. By 1980, the number of homes with at least one television had increased to 77.8 million with 39.7 homes owning two or more sets. In 1994, the number had reached 94.2 million homes with televisions; homes with more than one television fell to 35.8 million, perhaps because of the growing popularity of the VCR: 74.4 million homes owned a VCR in 1994.

When you consider that the number of homes with televisions in the U.S. is 98 percent of all households' population, you can see that Americans consider television an integral item in their lives.

But ownership only tells a small part of the story. The viewing habits of the average American family indicate more about television's scope of influence.

Listen to the following statistics. In 1950, the average number of television viewing hours per home was 4.58. The amount of daily viewing time per family steadily increased to 5.93 hours in 1970, 6.73 hours in 1980, and reached 6.88 hours in 1994.

The research shows that women watch the most television daily (with 4.42 hours per day), men come in second with 3.75 hours, teens watch an average of 2.77 hours per day, and children under age twelve watch the least, with 2.72 hours daily. (Children between ages one and two watch about 2 hours a day.)

Though children and teens watch less than adults, the amount of daily time devoted to television viewing is astounding. Think about the impact in the lives of children and teens over the span of a year or a lifetime. Statisticians estimate that in one year the average child watches 1,300 hours of television. By the age of eighteen, he or she will have watched 20,000 hours.

When do people watch the most television? No doubt the majority of the viewing is done during the hours of 8 to 11 P.M., the prime time hours. In 1994, the night with the most viewers watching during prime time was Wednesday, with nearly 95 million viewers. The weekend nights of Friday and Saturday drew the least viewers with 80.8 and 79 million viewers respectively.

When you consider the number of family hours per day spent in front of the television, you can begin to understand the influence that television holds in the modern American home. Think about any other item of property that most American homes have . . . say, for an example, a bicycle. Think of the difference in lives of the family members if they spent nearly seven daily hours riding a bicycle! (I'm sure the number of dieters across the U.S. would decline!) What if the item were a book . . . how would reading seven hours per day change your life, your goals, your ideas about your world?

The impact of such viewing on children is most likely greater than we can imagine. For example, as a result of the time spent in front of the television, families are likely to spend less time in conversation. Studies indicate that even the traditional time spent in family conversation, the dinner table, is affected by viewing habits. Thirty percent of all adults watch television during dinner.

Some say that television viewing is still a family activity, and it can lead to discussions arising from the issues and events portrayed on the TV. However, since nearly fifty percent of children between ages six and seventeen have a television set in their bedroom, we can presume that the children are watching alone and not under parental supervision. Parental supervision seems to be minimal. In fact, thirty-seven percent of parents do not set *any* limit on what their children view or how much their children watch.

So you can see, television holds a dominant position in our society. From the number of television sets owned to the hours viewed daily and the nature of that viewing, statistics show us that television is currently a great part of each of our lives.

And what of the future? We can assume that television will continue to hold a place of influence in the average American's life as more stations offer specialized programming and the influence of the growing telecommunications industry is felt. There are exciting new technological developments that will no doubt affect each of our lives. Watch and see!

References

Goleman, Daniel. "Studies Reveal TV's Potential to Teach Infants." *New York Times,* November 22, 1994, C1. Cited in J. Trelease, *The Read-Aloud Handbook.* New York: Penguin Books, 1995.

Monush, B. *1995 International Television and Video Almanac.* New York: Quigley Publishing Company, 1995.

"Parents Do Care." *Reading Today* (IRA bimonthly), February/March 1993, 22. Cited in J. Trelease, *The Read-Aloud Handbook.* New York: Penguin Books, 1995.

Trelease, J. *The Read-Aloud Handbook.* New York: Penguin Books, 1995.

"TV 'Profoundly' Influences Children's Lives, Survey Shows." Cox News Service, September 26, 1991. Based on Yankelovitch Youth Monitor national survey for Corporation for Public Broadcasting cited in J. Trelease, *The Read-Aloud Handbook.* New York: Penguin Books, 1995.